PASSION AND RESURRECTION NARRATIVES
(Chapters 18–21)

BY
JOHN S RUSSELL

This booklet is copyright and may not be copied or reproduced, in whole or part, by any means, without the publisher's prior written consent.

© Copyright 2002

Abacus Educational Services
424 Birmingham Road
Marlbrook
Bromsgrove
Worcestershire
B61 0HL

ISBN 1898653 24 0

Other titles available in this series:
1. Signs
2. Eschatology and Judgement
3. Holy Spirit
4. Discourses
5. Person and Work of Jesus

Also available:

Ethics series:
1. Ethical Theory and Language
2. Moral Rules
3. Christian Ethics (in preparation)
4. Homosexuality
5. Abortion
6. Euthanasia
7. Environmental Ethics

Philosophy of Religion series:
1. Religious Language
2. The Problem of Evil
3. Faith and Reason
4. God and Proof
5. Revelation and Religious Experience
6. Life after Death
7. Miracles
8. Freewill and Determinism

Philosophy series:
1. Philosophy of Mind (in preparation)

Other titles on the Synoptic Gospels are also available.

CONTENTS

INTRODUCTION	4
WHAT IS MEANT BY THE 'PASSION' AND 'RESURRECTION' 'NARRATIVES'?	5
THE SOURCE OF JOHN'S PASSION AND RESURRECTION NARRATIVES	6
PREPARING THE READER IN CHAPTER 1-17	7
THE 'GLORY' OF THE PASSION AND RESURRECTION OF JESUS	9
THE PASSION NARRATIVES:	11
THE ARREST IN THE GARDEN	11
THE TRIAL OF JESUS BEFORE ANNAS AND CAIAPHAS	17
PETER'S DENIALS	22
THE TRIAL OF JESUS BEFORE PILATE	24
THE CRUCIFIXION OF JESUS	30
THE BURIAL OF JESUS	37
THE RESURRECTION NARRATIVES:	39
THE EMPTY TOMB	39
THE APPEARANCE TO MARY MAGDALENE	41
THE FIRST APPEARANCE TO THE DISCIPLES	42
THE DOUBT OF THOMAS	44
THE SECOND APPEARANCE TO THE DISCIPLES (INCLUDING THOMAS)	44
CLOSING VERSES 20V30-31	46
THE APPEARANCE OF JESUS BY THE SEA OF GALILEE	47
SOME POSSIBLE PURPOSES OF THE PASSION AND RESURRECTION NARRATIVES	56
SYMBOLISM OR HISTORICITY?	65
WORKSHEET	68
EXAM QUESTIONS	69
FURTHER READING	74

INTRODUCTION

This series of booklets has been written specifically to cater for the needs of A/AS students of Religious Studies. However, it may equally be used as an introduction to areas of John's Gospel by the interested lay person or by first year undergraduates, especially those at Theological College.

The style of this booklet is similar to the others in this series and those on the Synoptic Gospels, containing consideration of the topic's main features, a worksheet, and a section on examination questions, making the booklet useful both for teaching and revision.

WHAT IS MEANT BY THE 'PASSION' AND RESURRECTION' 'NARRATIVES'?

The word 'Passion' in Biblical terms refers to the suffering and death of Jesus. In the Fourth Gospel this 'Passion' is related in Chapters 13-19, though the Passion 'Narrative' "does not begin until chapter 18" (The Gospel according to John, Carson, pg103), namely with Jesus' arrest in the garden. John refers to Jesus' 'Passion', and particularly the crucifixion, as Jesus' 'hour'. So the Passion 'Narrative' is the story of the actual events of Jesus' 'hour'. These events are Jesus' arrest, Jesus' trials before Annas and Caiaphas, Peter's denials, Jesus' trial before Pilate, Jesus' crucifixion and his burial.

The 'Resurrection' refers to Jesus' rising from the dead, and the Resurrection 'Narrative' is the sequence of events, which occurs after Jesus' burial. These incidents are found in Chapters 20-21, and include the Empty Tomb, and the appearances of Jesus to Mary Magdalene, to his disciples, to his disciples including Thomas, and to the seven disciples by the Sea of Galilee.

While the 'Passion' and 'Resurrection' of Jesus may be viewed separately, for the evangelist they also seem to be intertwined into one unit, "His death-and-resurrection, as one complete event." (The Interpretation of the Fourth Gospel, Dodd, pg439). In Chapters 1-17 the evangelist builds up to the final 'event', indicating on many occasions links with that 'event', and signposting the reader, to what itself may be a 'sign', the "supreme semeion" (The Gospel according to St. John, Barrett, pg65). (For further discussion, see Booklet 1 ('Signs') in this series).

This booklet on the Passion and Resurrection 'Narratives' particularly focuses on the events in Chapters 18-21. Comments on the Farewell Discourses of Jesus can be found in Booklet 4 ('Discourses') in this series.

THE 'SOURCE' OF JOHN'S PASSION AND RESURRECTION NARRRATIVES

There are various opinions on from where John obtained his Passion and Resurrection narratives. There seem to be three main suggestions. Firstly, that John used the Synoptic Gospels, or in particular Mark's Gospel, but that in his editing he used fresh material. Secondly, that John used a source that was independent but akin to, and influenced by, the Synoptic Gospels; the source contained similarities yet also some striking differences. Thirdly, that John acquired his material from a source totally independent of the Synoptic Gospels.

There is no general agreement on which is the most likely of these three alternatives. Occasionally scholars, aware of the difficulties in identifying John's possible source, or even his sources, refer to 'Tradition' used by John rather than labelling the material he used by the word 'source'.

Dodd suggests that the foundation for John's material lay within the 'kerygma' of the Early Church. 'Kerygma' refers to the actual 'preaching' of the initial disciples, and according to Dodd includes, the fulfilment of scripture, Jesus as the messiah descended from David, Jesus a performer of signs, and who was crucified but who rose from the dead. Yet Jesus ascended and was exalted to the right hand of God; Jesus would return (his 'Parousia'). In the meantime, the Holy Spirit was present within the Church, and people should repent and be baptised in order to obtain salvation and the Holy Spirit. ('Apostolic Preaching and its Development', Dodd, pgs26-29).

PREPARING THE READER IN CHAPTERS 1-17 FOR THE PASSION AND RESURRECTION NARRATIVES

In Chapter 2v2 Jesus announces that his hour 'has not yet come'. It is generally agreed that by his 'hour' Jesus (or the evangelist) was referring to his suffering and death upon the cross. If this is true then as early as Chapter 2 Jesus' is focusing on the time when he will sacrifice himself on that cross.

Later in the same chapter (v19) Jesus indicates that if they destroy the temple he will build it again in three days. His audience take his words to apply literally to the temple building in Jerusalem, but the evangelist links Jesus' words to the 'temple of his body', and thus to its 'destruction' on the cross, but its subsequent raising after three days. At the time, even his disciples were not aware of Jesus' intended meaning, but following Jesus' resurrection they recalled his words.

In Chapter 3v14 the evangelist refers to the 'lifting up' of Jesus, as Son of man. This is generally interpreted as referring to Jesus being lifted up on the cross. The evangelist wishes to suggest that this lifting up was so that believers should have life, though paradoxically through the death of Jesus.

In Chapter 4 Jesus heals the Officer's son. The son is 'at the point of death' (v47) and it is possible that the evangelist has in mind the future events of Jesus where he is likewise at the point of death, but from where he actually goes on to die. So if there is a link with Jesus' fate at this point, there is also clearly a contrast.

The evangelist mentions that on a number of occasions (e.g. 5v18, 7v25, and 8v40) the Jews wished to kill Jesus, and in 11v53 that the Jewish authorities took counsel and began planning to take away Jesus' life. Also in Chapter 13v21 Jesus indicates that one of his disciples will betray him.

Yet the evangelist considered that Jesus was actually going to 'lay down his life' rather than it be taken away, and that he was to give his life as a good shepherd would lay down his life to protect his sheep. While Jesus' soul was troubled (12v27) because of his impending doom, he was unwilling to ask his Father to save him from his 'hour', as it was for this very purpose that he had come from the Father. In 15v13 it is suggested that to die for ones friends was the pinnacle of love.

In Chapter 11 Lazarus dies, which may be a foreshadowing of Jesus' own death. In Chapter 12 Mary, Lazarus' sister, anoints Jesus which is done for the day of Jesus' burial. (12v7). In Chapter 16 Jesus is aware that in a little while his disciples will see him no more (16v16) and in consequence they are full of sorrow (16v22).

Yet for the evangelist, Jesus is the grain of wheat that dies in order to bear fruit (12v24), and through his death, and being lifted up onto the cross, he will bring believers to life (3v14). This 'life (in Greek 'zoe aionios') is 'eternal life', which fundamentally is a 'knowing', a relationship with the Father and Jesus himself (17v3).

Yet Jesus' death is not the end, but merely a stage preparing for his resurrection. Indeed it is possible that when the evangelist talks of Jesus being lifted up he means lifted up in resurrection, and possibly also ascension, to be with the Father again. So in Chapter 2 when Jesus talks of his hour, the evangelist is also aware that Jesus will rise. The officer's son (Chapter 4) is healed by Jesus, and the narrative's crux becomes the son's living rather than a focus on his dying.

Jesus not only lays down his life but he also has the power to take it up again (10v17-18), and this may be foreshadowed when Lazarus is raised in Chapter 11. While the disciples are sad because they will see him no more, they are reassured that they will see him in a little while and because he will come to them (14v18) they will have joy. It may be that the evangelist also sees the coming of the Paraclete, (as Jesus is to return to the Father), as the spiritual return, the alter ego, of Jesus.

An appreciation of this preparatory material in chapters 1-17, may enable the reader to gain a better understanding of the Passion and Resurrection narratives of Chapters 18-21.

THE 'GLORY' OF THE PASSION AND RESURRECTION OF JESUS

While the evangelist throughout his gospel shows the humanity of Jesus, the emphasis on Jesus' person appears to be on his 'special' nature. Jesus is the unique Son of God, who has come from above and will return to that realm. The evangelist repeatedly suggests links of Jesus with the Father; for him Jesus is Logos and can use the divine 'I am' because he shares that divinity with the Father (See Booklet 5 in this series).

In Chapter 1v14 the evangelist does state that the Logos became flesh in the person of Jesus, but even in the same verse he goes on to mention Jesus' 'glory'. This 'glory' is a feature of the gospel, and is clearly of major significance for the evangelist.

Jesus seeks the Father's glory, but also the Father as judge seeks Jesus' glory; indeed the Father himself glorifies Jesus (8v54). The evangelist records in the Raising of Lazarus incident that 'This illness is not unto death; it is for the glory of God, so that the Son of God may be glorified by means of it.' (11v4). Clearly the evangelist wishes to demonstrate the glory of Jesus, and this is true for the evangelist even in Jesus' crucifixion. While the cross in Mark's Gospel may be linked with the humiliation, defeat, and despair of Jesus, in the Fourth Gospel it is that supreme moment when the glory of Jesus shines brightest. Jesus is lifted up on the cross to divine glory. He will later be lifted up in the resurrection and ascension, but for the evangelist he is glorified and exalted in death.

In Chapter 13 Jesus acts as a servant when he washes the disciples feet, yet immediately Judas has gone out into the night (v30) to betray Jesus to the authorities, Jesus sees his glorification is 'now' as the Son of man, for the Father will 'glorify him at once.' (13v32). The Paraclete too, as part of his role, will glorify Jesus (16v14). This Holy Spirit itself will not be given until Jesus has been glorified, but in 20v22 Jesus breathes on his disciples the Holy Spirit, which by implication means that Jesus has therefore been glorified, and this through the cross-and-resurrection event.

In Chapter 17, the chapter immediately before the Passion narrative proper, there is much emphasis on 'glory'. The reason for this is that Jesus' 'hour has come' (v1), and it is in Jesus' death-and-resurrection that his glorification will be achieved. So Jesus prays that the Father will now glorify the Son (v1), and in God's 'own presence with the glory which I (Jesus) had with thee before the world was made.' (v5). Jesus is glorified in the disciples (v10), and he prays that they in turn will 'behold my glory which thou hast given me in thy love for me before the foundation of the world.' (v24).

This glory, Jesus' shining majesty, will be demonstrated to the disciples in the cross and resurrection; later it will shine forth when he returns to the Father, and Jesus desires that his disciples should 'be with me where I am' (v24) to experience his glorification.

THE PASSION NARRATIVES:
▶THE ARREST IN THE GARDEN (18v1-12)

The Chapter begins by indicating that when Jesus "had spoken these words" he went to a garden. 'These words' refers to his prayer in chapter 17, where he had prayed for himself, his disciples, and all future believers. He had particularly prayed about his glory and for the protection and the sanctification (holiness) of his disciples. The prayer ends with an indication that they will see Jesus' glory, and that God's love may be in them, and that Jesus himself may be in them, indicating a relationship of mutual indwelling.

In John's Gospel there is no prayer in the garden itself. In the Synoptic Gospels Jesus prays to avoid the impending doom, though only if that is the wish of the Father. In the Fourth gospel the prayer in Chapter 17 precedes the garden incident but there is 'no anguished prayer' ('The Gospel of John', Grayston, John pg150), and certainly no fear or wobbling, no 'moment of weakness' ('John', Beasley-Murray, pg381). Jesus realises his task has to be accomplished before he returns to the Father.

So, in John, Jesus goes forward, accompanied by his disciples, into a garden across the Kidron Valley, which was to the east of the city of Jerusalem. Jesus had previously entered the city to popular acclaim, he now goes out to his arrest.

The garden is referred to in Mark and Matthew as Gethsemane (meaning 'oil press'). The garden may have been an olive grove or even a walled enclosure (Carson pg576) in which possibly grew herbs or vegetables. For Jesus it was a meeting place, a place where he had 'often met' with his disciples. Judas knew this, and "this explains why the traitor could find Jesus." ('The Gospel according to St. John', Schnackenburg, pg222).

In verse 3, John records how Judas had procured a group of men to arrest Jesus. A number of motives have been assigned to Judas for his betrayal of his master. These include almost semi-noble reasons, such as Judas wished to force Jesus into openly revealing himself as an earthly Messiah. Yet in John's Gospel, Judas is painted with dark brushstrokes. In Chapter 12 he is declared a thief, stealing money from the communal purse; so the motive of greed might be intended for the betrayal. In Chapter 13 Judas is entered by Satan, and Judas goes from Jesus' presence into the darkness, as John tellingly records 'It was night.'

Judas now comes at night to effect the arrest of Jesus. Darkness in the Fourth Gospel represents a time of unenlightenment but also of evil and sin. In contrast followers of Jesus walk in the light, as he himself is he 'light of the world'. For the evangelist Judas may symbolise one who is in darkness, the night man. Perhaps there is Johannine irony in the description that Judas and his gang need to come with artificial lanterns and torches to arrest the one who for the evangelist is the 'light of the world'. Brown comments (The Gospel according to John Vol. 2, pg817) that there is "direct confrontation of Jesus and the forces of darkness."

John records that the arresting group included soldiers and some officers from the Chief Priests and Pharisees. It is generally maintained that the evangelist intends to show that the soldiers were Roman soldiers and were involved together with the temple police in the arrest of Jesus. If this is so it would indicate a pre-arrest collusion between the Jewish authorities and Roman authorities, with Pilate possibly "tipped off to Jesus' arrest" (Carson, pg577).

Jesus had frequently upset the Jews by such things as cleansing the temple, acting against their laws, and creating a following through performing signs. Collusion with the Romans to arrest Jesus would rid the Jews of their 'opponent' and ensure that they were not implicated in his actions, which could cause a potential threat from the Romans. Also Jesus could be a threat to Roman rule and peace if he had a large following and was recognised and acclaimed as a messianic king. Thus the arresting group come armed with weapons. Trouble had to be avoided at Passover when Jerusalem was overcrowded with Jews.

The 'officers' were sent by the Chief priests and Pharisees. The Chief priests were "generally Sadducees" ('Jerusalem in the time of Jesus', Jeremias, pg230), and many high ranking priests would be members of the Jewish Sanhedrin, the supreme Jewish assembly and court in the land. The priesthood was also in control of the temple and had authority over the temple police. The Pharisees were laymen, largely from the middle class. They were driven by their meticulous zeal for the Law. Many of the lawyers were understandably Pharisees, and these too could be members of the Sanhedrin. Jeremias (pg232) notes that the power of the Pharisees grew stronger in the first half of the First Century AD as the importance of the Sadducees declined. Here the 'authorities' work together, and even with the Romans. While the Pharisees were not noted for their support of Roman rule, clearly they were prepared to put their differences aside in order that Jesus might be killed. After this point the Pharisees are not mentioned again in the gospel, though the Chief Priests, and the High Priest, will have further parts to play in the saga.

In verse 4 it is stated that Jesus was aware of all that was to happen to him. This 'knowingness', "Jesus' suprahuman knowledge" (Schnackenburg pg223) is a feature within the gospel, "a strong Johannine theme." (Brown, pg809). It may merely suggest the prophetic awareness of Jesus, but it could also suggest omniscience and hence be linking Jesus with divinity. Yet Jesus does not shirk the task known to him and unafraid 'came forward' presenting himself openly to his enemies. He does not seek to avoid arrest nor does he try to escape. Beasley-Murray (pg320) considers that the accusations of Celsus, (an early pagan opponent of Christianity), that Jesus tried to escape arrest, may be actively opposed in the evangelist's narrative. Judas has no part in showing the arresting group which person is Jesus; according to the Synoptic Gospels Judas did this by kissing his master. It is Jesus himself who asks, 'Whom do you seek?', and when they reply, 'Jesus of Nazareth' he reveals himself to them with 'I am he.'

For the evangelist this may be more than a simple indication 'that's me'; it may be the revelation that Jesus is divine, recalling Exodus 3v6, where Yahweh (God) tells Moses that he is 'I am what I am', "the God of Israel's self-identifying affirmation" ('The Gospel of John', Bruce, pg341). Sanders and Mastin ('According to St. John', pg 385) suggest Jesus' words emphasise his divine majesty, (his glory), while Marsh ('Saint John', pg582) suggests there are divine overtones in his words. In the Fourth Gospel there are many occasions where

Jesus' self-identification, as 'I am', is accompanied by some qualifying material. For example Jesus states 'I am the light of the world' and 'I am the bread of life'. Previously when Jesus used 'I am he' he was revealing himself as the Messiah to the Samaritan woman (4v26).

In 18v5 John records that Judas was standing with the arresting group, the "powers of darkness" (Sanders and Mastin pg385). Judas has only a passive role, not speaking or coming to kiss Jesus. This does not exonerate Judas (Carson pg578), and there is certainly no place in the Johannine account for the Matthaean remorse of Judas, his attempts to make amends for his treachery, or the account of him then committing suicide. Judas, together with the arresting party, is simply described as drawing back and falling to the ground (v6) because Jesus has said 'I am he'. "The arresting group sinking before the epiphany of Deity" ('The Gospel of John', Bultmann, pg639) for the evangelist may be the appropriate reaction, almost one of obeisance before Jesus, thus indicating his majesty and divinity; he "displays enough of his glory that they fall backwards to the ground." (Carson pg572). Brown (pg818) considers "there is little doubt John intended 'I am' as a divine name" showing Jesus' divine "power over the forces of darkness."

Yet Jesus is also presented as the human being that is to be arrested and eventually executed. In verse 7 Jesus asks again whom they seek, and to their answer of 'Jesus of Nazareth', he adds, 'I told you I am he'. He is not concerned for his own safety; rather he requests that his followers be allowed to go free. This is the concern for his disciples' safety that he voiced to the Father in his prayer in Chapter 17. It is also his desire that his own words that he has spoken in Chapter 6v39, 'lost not one', and in Chapter 17v12 'lost not one except the son of perdition' (i.e. Judas himself) should be fulfilled. Generally in scripture it is God's words that are fulfilled; for the evangelist Jesus may be speaking the divine words.

Jesus is bargaining his own life for the freedom of his followers. Barrett ('The Gospel according to St. John', pg520) writes of Jesus buying the disciples' safety with his own life, thereby acting out the Good Shepherd parable; Jesus is the true Good Shepherd laying down his life for his friends. Jesus is portrayed as giving himself rather than being taken (Dodd pg426). It may be implied that the bargaining is accepted, as the disciples are not arrested.

Yet before Jesus is arrested Simon Peter appears to make a valiant attempt to protect his master and prevent the arrest. While the Synoptic Gospels record that 'one of the disciples' used his sword, cutting off the ear of the High Priest's servant, John names that disciple as Simon Peter. Peter may be brave but this is impetuosity that Jesus does not require. Jesus may be concerned that his disciples are allowed to go thereby fulfilling his words, which may not happen if there is a fight with weapons. However, Jesus' words of rebuke to Peter, 'Put your sword into its sheath', more pertinently occur as Jesus must drink the cup which his Father has given him (v11). This is the cup of suffering which the Synoptic Gospels record Jesus had wanted taken away from him. This is not so for John. The evangelist, in what may be an allusion to the synoptic wobbling of Jesus, in Chapter 12v27 states that Jesus was sorely troubled, but he was not to ask the Father to save him from this hour because it was his purpose to come to this hour. So in Chapter 18 Jesus (Barrett pg522) makes a calm determined acceptance of the cup, and thus (Sanders and Mastin pg387) a confident acceptance of his destiny.

Jesus tells Simon Peter to put away his sword. To portray a Jesus encouraging his followers to fight would of course suggest he was a political rebel or political Messiah, so Jesus immediately checks any such resistance (Bruce pg342). For the evangelist Jesus is no earthly king who desired his followers to fight to save him as his later words to Pilate (18v36) clearly show. Peter has acted against Jesus' desires and Peter's action is "a tactic ... as pointless as Peter's misunderstanding is total...a denial of the work to which Jesus consecrated himself." (Carson pg579). Peter, with characteristic misunderstanding and error, is showing "human understanding which does not grasp God's plan." (Schnackenburg pg27).

John, in agreement with Luke, records Peter cut off the 'right' ear of the High Priest's servant, though unlike Luke there is no record of Jesus healing the ear. This would be an action Barrett (pg522) thinks would have been inappropriate for John, as "the gulf between Jesus and his adversaries, between light and darkness, was now unbridgeable." The Fourth Gospel's account also differs from Luke in that John actually names the High Priest's servant as Malchus. It may be that the account of an eyewitness is behind the details of the garden arrest. For some this is likely to be the Beloved Disciple uniquely referred to in John's Gospel, and seemingly identified as the author of the gospel in Chapter 21v24.

The name Malchus actually transliterates into the word 'king'. It seems possible that here is the Johannine characteristic feature of irony. Peter fights against 'king' Malchus as he has the earthly vision of protecting 'king' Jesus. A 'double entendre' may also be intended in that Peter is actually fighting against the intentions of 'king Jesus'.

Another possible characteristic feature of the Fourth Gospel is John's interest in symbolism. John's account of the arrest has been thought to have such possible symbolic intentions, namely in his reference to the place being a 'garden'. Could there be an intentional link with the 'garden' of Eden, rather than just a record of some actual garden? Brown (pg806) is unconvinced by arguments for a link with Eden as he notes the Greek word for garden in John is 'kepos' not the 'paradeisos' (Paradise) of the Genesis story.

Yet if John's intention was to symbolise the Garden of Eden, how is the symbolism to be interpreted? It is possible that John may have in mind that Jesus is the new Adam, and one contrasting with Adam in Eden. There Adam was disobedient to God, hid himself from God, and brought sin and death into the world. In the Gospel Jesus is obedient to his Father's wishes even if that means dying, he openly reveals himself, and will die to free mankind of the responsibility for sin. Judas may be representative of the devil. The evangelist has already linked Judas with Satan. In Chapter 6v70-71 the betrayer is said to be a devil; in Chapter 13v2 Satan is said to have put it into Judas' heart to betray Jesus, and in v27 Satan entered Judas.

There are certain problems with such an analogy. For example, who represents Eve? Perhaps John cannot have a woman in the garden incident as that would be against tradition. Yet John has some unique features in his story. It could be that Peter's action represents Eve's attempts at temptation, to try to encourage or force Jesus to enter a battle with his opponents and establish himself as the messianic conqueror of Jewish expectation. Though it may sound a little harsh, Peter might even himself represent Satan. It may also be that Peter, rather than Jesus, is in fact Adam, but one who like the first Adam errs in understanding and action, though he seems braver than the hiding Adam bewitched by Eve.

A further problem might be raised when one considers how John seems to present Jesus as the all-knowing revealing 'I am'. That might then lead to the interpretation that Jesus is God in Eden to be betrayed and disobeyed by evil Satan and his henchmen, whoever it is that one equates Satan to in the Johannine material.

In verse 12 Jesus is seized and bound by 'the band of soldiers and their captain and the officers of the Jews'.

A summary of impressions of the arrest in the garden

- Jesus is in control of events within the garden.
- He gives himself to those coming to arrest him though knowing that he is then to die.
- Jesus is linked with the divine 'I am'.
- He bargains for the freedom of his followers.
- Peter acts against the desire of Jesus that his words may be fulfilled and that he may drink the cup of suffering.
- There may be symbolism and irony in John's presentation (for example, the lanterns, Peter being the one to cut off 'Malchus' ear', and the 'garden').
- Characteristic features – light and darkness, Jesus' knowingness, the divine links of Jesus, Peter's misunderstanding and errors, irony, and symbolism.

▶ THE TRIALS OF JESUS BEFORE ANNAS AND CAIAPHAS (18v13-14, v19-24, v28)

The arresting group firstly take Jesus to Annas. This incident is unique to John's Gospel. John notes that Annas was the father-in-law of Caiaphas. Both Annas (6-15AD) and Caiaphas (18-36 AD – though

Jeremias argues pg195 for 37AD) served as High Priests. Indeed until 41AD the family of Annas had a virtual monopoly of the High Priesthood (Sanders and Mastin pg388). While Caiaphas is mentioned as High Priest for that year (v13) this does not necessarily suggest that the evangelist saw the office as a yearly tenure. In verse 14 John reminds us that "it was Caiaphas who had given counsel to the Jews that it was expedient that one man should die for the people". This clearly reflects the passage Chapter 11v49-53 in which it was decided Jesus should die as many believed in him through his raising of Lazarus from the dead.

The trial material is broken up by v15-18 with the initial denial by Peter, but in verse 19-24 Jesus is actually questioned by "the High Priest". This reference may be slightly confusing as Jesus is now to be interrogated by Annas and previously John had stated Caiaphas was High Priest that year. It seems this interrogation must be before Annas as in verse 24 Annas then 'sent him bound to Caiphas'. It may be that the confusion is caused by the evangelist's belief that Annas could still be regarded as High Priest though his actual tenure was over. Annas held a patriarchal position and Sanders and Mastin (pg 389) comment that the title High Priest could, from respect, also be given to an ex-High Priest. This might be particularly so of Annas. Valerius Gratus, Pilate's predecessor, had deposed Annas. This did not mean his influence would then cease as according to Mosaic Law a person was to be High Priest for life (Carson pg580), and Annas may have been held to be the 'true' High Priest by many as he had been deposed by the foreign power of Rome. It is possible that Annas was the power behind Caiaphas, thus retaining his title and his authority.

The meeting before Annas hardly seems to be a trial; it is more a questioning of Jesus. Thus Annas would not have been constrained by legalities governing a trial. He could interrogate Jesus at night and ask leading questions of the defendant. Even if it were an actual trial, Carson remarks (pg583) that legal loopholes could be found. The actual questioning centres on Jesus' general teaching and his disciples, though the evangelist records no detailed questions. Jesus response demonstrates that he was not part of some secret society, nor involved in a conspiracy (Carson pg583) against the interests of both Jews and Romans. Jesus had spoken openly to the world, acting as a teacher both in synagogues and the temple. The Jewish synagogue was the local meeting place for worship and there were many synagogues. There was only one temple, in Jerusalem, and it was the centre of Jewish worship and the sacrificial system. Jesus states that in such places "all Jews come together" perhaps again emphasising nothing has been done or said in secret. So open is Jesus' teaching that he states the Jews have heard him speak so they should be asked what they know; Jesus "is denying any secret and subversive activity and demanding that they produce witnesses prepared to testify on oath in open court." ('The Priority of John', Robinson, pg249).

In reality Jesus seems to be instructing his interrogators on how to carry out a fair trial and how they should seek the witness (a characteristic feature in the gospel) and testimony of those who have heard Jesus' words so that all may be presented in evidence. His words are taken as insolence by one of the officers, presumably as it is taken that he has cursed the chief of the people which is against the instruction in Exodus 22v28. The officer asks if that is how to answer the High Priest, and then he strikes Jesus. Carson notes (pg 584) that the Greek word for 'struck' is rhapisma which means a sharp blow with the flat of the hand. Of course this action is also improper and so Jesus, undeterred by violence, again instructs them on legal proceedings; if he has spoken wrongly the witnesses should state the case, while if he has spoken rightly, why is he being struck?

The 'trial' then ends abruptly, and John states that "Annas then sent him bound to Caiaphas the High Priest." Verses 25-27 deal with Peter's further denials. In verse 28 John records, "Then they led Jesus from the house of Caiaphas". So there are no details whatsoever of the trial before Caiaphas. This is at least unexpected when one considers the account of the trial before Caiaphas and the Sanhedrin in the Synoptic Gospels, where Caiaphas is shown to be the prime mover and villain of the proceedings in finding Jesus guilty of blasphemy and worthy of death. Generally, commentators on John's Gospel, also link the evangelist with this presentation of Caiaphas as the villain. Yet an analysis of the Caiaphas material in the Fourth Gospel questions that assumption.

John presumably has good reason for not including what in tradition must have been an important incident. Barrett (pg 523) questions, though without answer, why we hear nothing of the result of the examination before Caiaphas, noting "The Jewish trial is glossed over" though "one has to presume than an examination likewise took place before Caiaphas." (Bultmannn pg642). It is possible that John felt it so well known he did just gloss over it. It is also true that Caiaphas earlier in Chapter 11v49ff judged that it was expedient that Jesus should die. Yet in that passage Caiaphas had declared it "expedient" for Jesus to die in order to safeguard the Jewish nation from perishing. The one had to be sacrificed for the many. Caiaphas is actually stating that it is 'appropriate' for Jesus to die; it is the sensible and easiest action to take in the circumstances. The circumstance apparently being that the Romans might attack the Jews if Jesus remained alive and active. John does not have Caiaphas stating it is 'right' to execute Jesus, merely "expedient".

What John does further record in 11v51 is that Caiaphas "did not say this of his own accord, but being High Priest that year he prophesied that Jesus should die". This seems to hint that Jesus' death was not what he himself might actually want, but as High Priest he had to serve the interest of the Jews in general. The implication would then be that had he not been High Priest he would not even have counselled that Jesus should die.

In 11v52 the evangelist records that Caiaphas' prophecy was that Jesus should not die "for the nation only, but to gather into one the children of God who are scattered abroad." The truth of this latter comment is one of the central tenets of Christianity, and John records it was Caiaphas who appreciated it. He it is who seemingly shows appreciative prophetic skills, though it is possible the evangelist is merely using his editorial skills, perhaps to create irony.

It seems possible to argue that the picture John is painting of Caiaphas is somewhat sympathetic. Perhaps this possible intention is behind the absence later in Chapter 18 of a detailed account of the trial before Caiaphas. In John Annas becomes the villain of the piece, though it is true that Caiaphas actually hands Jesus over to the Romans, which in due course leads to Jesus' execution. If there is then the possibility of a sympathetic presentation of Caiaphas, what could the evangelist's purpose be?

In Chapter 18v15, (part of the 'Peter's denials' material considered below), John records how the disciple accompanying Peter was "known to the High Priest" and was able to enter the court of the High Priest. Again Caiaphas is not shown as anti-Jesus. It is possible that Caiaphas was not aware of his acquaintance being a disciple, but this seems unlikely as the disciple is known as such by the "maid who kept the door (v16f).

It seems arguable that the treatment of Caiaphas is part of some Johannine 'apologetic' to suggest not all of the authorities were really anti-Jesus. Even in the interrogation before Annas there is no animosity from Annas himself, nor is a guilty verdict actually pronounced. Sanders and Mastin (pg 391) suggests the trial before Annas actually reflected the trials of later Christians, which would again be part of the Johannine 'apologetic'.

A further purpose of the evangelist is also possible. The 'another disciple' of verse 15 is generally argued as being the Beloved Disciple, uniquely referred to in the Fourth Gospel. Later in Chapter 21v24 the Beloved Disciple is referred to as the witness behind the Gospel and its author. So the evangelist is the Beloved Disciple/another disciple, and hence himself the friend of Caiaphas. However, if this was openly stated it could reflect badly on the evangelist, given the accepted traditional actions of Caiaphas, and thus on the gospel itself. Perhaps John has doubly veiled the identity of the Beloved Disciple by the reference to the "another disciple', and removed the anti-Caiaphas material in order to avoid such hostility to his gospel.

A summary of impressions of the Jewish trials

- There is a very brief trial before Annas.
- Jesus is merely asked about his disciples and teaching.
- It is established that Jesus is a teacher and one working openly.
- John presents veiled criticism of the way the authorities interrogate Jesus as they do not follow the correct procedures.

- There is mere mention, without details, of Jesus being sent to Caiaphas – possibly part of a sympathetic treatment of Caiaphas.
- Characteristic features – witness, and Jesus being innocent (of subversion).

▶ PETER'S DENIALS (18v15-18, 25-28)

The material about Peter's denials is structured around the Jewish trial before Annas. The evangelist moves from one to the other in a dramatic presentation and possibly contrasting the denials of Peter with the openness and truth of Jesus. Peter is the liar, while Jesus is the Truth. There may also be contrast with Jesus' 'I am' in Gethsmane with the 'I am not' of Peter in his denials.

Yet it should be noted that Peter at least 'followed' Jesus (v15), which in the Fourth Gospel seems acquainted with the allegiance of discipleship. He follows in the company of 'another disciple'. It is a mystery who this disciple is (Beasley-Murray pg324). His anonymity may be a deliberate ploy of the evangelist, particularly if this disciple is the Beloved Disciple, for then there would be double anonymity, to cover up the identity of a friend of the High Priest (as discussed above). The disciple is 'known' to the High Priest, the Greek word 'gnostos' suggesting (Carson pg580) real friendship and possible intimacy. Peter only manages to gain entry to the courtyard through this disciple. Barrett (pg525) hints that the evangelist may introduce the 'another disciple' in order to explain how Peter could have entered the courtyard. Elsewhere in the gospel the Beloved Disciple is to be found in the company of Peter, but this relationship will be discussed later.

Peter is challenged at the gate by the maid there. She asks if he is also one of Jesus' disciples, presumably expecting the answer 'yes' as Peter accompanies a man who is clearly known as being a disciple of Jesus. Yet Peter says he is not and (Carson pg583) begins his shameful descent. Peter in verse 18 is standing with Jesus' opponents sharing the warmth of a charcoal fire, for his 'I am not' has separated him from Jesus. Judas too had stood with Jesus' enemies in the garden.

The denial's material is taken up again in verse 25 after the trial, with the repetition that Peter was warming himself. He denied for a second time when asked if he was a disciple of Jesus. The situation for Peter then becomes even trickier as a kinsman of Malchus, who Peter had attacked in the garden, says to Peter, 'Did I not see you in the garden with him?' Earlier in the garden Peter had been willing to face danger for Jesus, but not now. He denied for the third time and (v27) 'at once the cock crowed.' John's account finishes at this point, a dramatic ending particularly if Jesus' earlier words in Chapter 13v38 are remembered, for Jesus' prophecy of Peter's denial is fulfilled. Peter's earlier bravado has now evaporated as he believes he is at risk. This faithlessness contrasts again with the fearlessness of Jesus (Beasley-Murray pg324)

According to the Synoptic gospels, Peter remembered Jesus' words that he would deny his master, and from remorse he went out and wept bitterly. Yet in John's account there is no indication of Peter realising his mistake or thus being affected by it. There is the possibility that this omission is because the evangelist wishes to paint a more unsympathetic picture of Peter than do the synoptic writers. Marsh suggests (pg593) that John may end at the cockcrow for artistry and theological power.

A summary of impressions of Peter's denials

- Peter only gains entrance to the courtyard through the intervention of 'another disciple'.
- The 'another disciple' is an acquaintance of the High Priest.
- Simon Peter denies Jesus three times, fulfilling Jesus' earlier prophecy.
- John places Peter by a charcoal fire with Jesus' opponents – Peter seems to have separated himself from Jesus and his followers.
- There is no account of Peter realising what he has done or of any remorse.
- The evangelist may be contrasting Jesus and Peter for dramatic effect.
- Characteristic features – Peter's errors, and Jesus knowingness as his previous prophecy about Peter is fulfilled.

▶ THE TRIAL OF JESUS BEFORE PILATE (18v28-19v16)

The trial of Jesus before Pilate is quite a long passage that presents detailed discussion both between Pilate and Jesus and Pilate and the Jews. While it is possible that Pilate's private discussions with Jesus may have been later told to the disciples by the resurrected Jesus, or by the Holy Spirit, some scholars question the actual historicity of the material. Carson (pg587) wonders if the material is creative writing to make theological points, though "not necessarily ex nihilo (from nothing); Grayston (pg153) suggests John is writing a theological presentation in the form of a story.

The trial takes place 'early'; clearly Pilate is about his business promptly. He was the governor, or more correctly the Prefect, over Judaea from 26-36AD. Jesus is brought before him at the Praetorium. Pilate's usual headquarters were in Caesarea, but he went up to Jerusalem for the festivals. It is debated whether the Praetorium was in Herod's palace or in the Antonia fortress, but the "building where he (Pilate) took up temporary residence would be his praetorium for the time being." (Bruce pg348).

John initially (v28) records that the 'they' who took Jesus to Pilate did not themselves enter the Praetorium 'so that they might not be defiled, but might eat the passover'. This may again be the feature of Johannine irony, as they "plot to crucify the Son of God yet are scrupulous to the extreme about their own religious observances." (Marsh pg595); they want to eat the Passover lamb yet "demand the death of the Lamb of God ." (Beasley-Murray pg328). Fortna ('The Fourth Gospel and its predecessor', pg167) suggests that there may here be "Johannine polarity between God and the world….dramatically represented here as polarity between Jesus inside the Praetorium, and 'the Jews' outside."

As they want to eat the Passover meal it means that according to John Jesus is on trial and later crucified before Passover. The Synoptic Gospels record these events on the day of Passover, Nisan 15 in the Jewish calendar; yet for John the events happen on the day of preparation, Nisan 14.

According to John's presentation of Pilate, the prefect seems very accommodating to the Jews. They don't have to enter the Praetorium, but he himself keeps moving from inside the Praetorium to outside, to the awaiting Jews. Barrett notes (pg533) that Josephus' writings about Pilate would not lead one to expect such accommodating compliance. Yet it may have been wise for Pilate not to deliberately upset the Jews at Passover when so many Jews were in Jerusalem. Pilate may have been cruel when he wanted to be but he always seemed to act in his own best interests.

The movement of Pilate from outside to inside and vice-versa a number of times through the proceedings also may intentionally be to heighten the drama, producing "dramatic power" (Grayston pg153). It also means that the Jews are not in a place to hear Pilate's conversations with Jesus. Some scholars, from a narrative criticism perspective also see the action in stage-like terms with Pilate going back and forward to the front and rear of the stage (Carson pg589). Pilate is the only character in all of the 'scenes'.

Initially he is outside and asks what accusation they bring against Jesus. This seems strange if as earlier suggested as a possibility the Jews and Romans had colluded in the arrest of Jesus. It may be Pilate merely wanted to ratify the proceedings, but it did seem to "open up a new trial" (Grayston pg596). The question may therefore have been unexpected by the Jewish authorities, and this may produce what appears to be rudeness to Pilate on their part as they state 'If this man were not an evildoer, we would not have handed him over.' (18v30). The evangelist himself would have disagreed with the description of Jesus as an evildoer, and so would the whole early church, which viewed Jesus as the sinless (unblemished) Passover lamb.

Pilate tells them to take Jesus and judge him by their own law, and hence places the onus on them and attempts to relinquish the case. The Jews, as they are now described by the evangelist (v31), need Pilate, as they want Jesus executed and they are not permitted according to the evangelist's record, 'to put any man to death.' There continues to be debate, or "dispute" (Carson pg591) over whether in fact the Jews could themselves execute prisoners. The later stoning of Stephen in Acts Chapter 7 is cited to support their right to execute, but Grayston (pg 155) remarks that for the Sanhedrin to exercise capital jurisdiction would have been an exception rather than the rule for a local authority in a province. The evangelist sees their desire to execute Jesus as a fulfilment of Jesus' words.

The scene changes as Pilate enters the Praetorium to actually begin his interrogation of Jesus. Initially he asks Jesus if he is the king of the Jews. Perhaps this is the accusation made by the Jews against Jesus, though John has not previously indicated such a charge. Jesus immediately asks Pilate a question as to whether Pilate has said this of his own accord or has been told by others. This is the beginning of a discussion that develops on the kingship of Jesus, an emphasised feature within this section. Indeed Brown (pg863) comments that "kingship is the theological motif that dominates the episodes of the trial." The fact that Jesus is asking questions almost suggests a reversal of roles between Jesus and Pilate, with the scene "dominated by Jesus as king and the nature of sovereignty." (Beasley-Murray pg327), and with the possible irony, as it seems Pilate is on trial rather than Jesus.

Pilate answers Jesus' question with the words 'Am I a Jew?' (18v35). Clearly the answer to the question would be 'no'; this serves to clearly separate Pilate from the Jews. He points out that Jesus' own nation have delivered him to Pilate, though he also particularly singles out the Chief Priests. The discussion about kingship establishes that Jesus is no earthly king, though he most certainly is king. "Jesus interprets his kingship spiritually as not of this world." ('John – Evangelist and Interpreter', Smalley, pg201). Jesus further emphasises the non-earthly nature of his kingship by stating his followers would fight to stop him being handed over to the Jews if he was an earthly king. Of course this is actually what Peter had previously done in the garden, but his action had been criticised and stopped by the words of Jesus himself.

Jesus' denial of an earthly interest in sovereignty also removes his kingship from the sphere of sedition and rebellion (Barrett pg536) and also implies "Christianity's political innocence" (Barrett pg538). Yet he has used the word king, so Pilate asks him if he is then a king? Jesus states that king is actually Pilate's word, but Jesus has been born into the world in order to bear witness to truth. Here Jesus' birth is "unambiguously mentioned" (Carson pg594), though there is the implication that he has come from elsewhere. Pilate's response is to question 'What is truth?' (18v38). Of course for the evangelist the answer to this question is that Jesus is himself the truth, and while the presentation of Pilate is as one with a sense of fair play and openness, "yet he is of the world not of truth" (Barrett pg538).

Pilate returns outside to the Jews and the next scene begins. The apparent characteristic feature of Jesus' innocence, which the evangelist wishes to present, is demonstrated as Pilate tells the Jews that he finds Jesus innocent of any crime, but he raises himself (in Mark's Gospel it is the crowd) the custom of releasing a prisoner at Passover. The historicity of this custom has been questioned as there is no extra-Biblical evidence for it. It also might seem strange to release political criminals who were a threat to the state. Yet if it were just one prisoner on one occasion per year, and a gesture to the Jews at Passover when 'freedom' would be a major feature, it just could be historically acceptable. Pilate seems to do Jesus no favour by asking if they want him to release the king of the Jews. The Jews respond they don't want Jesus, they want Barabbas set free. John points out that Barabbas was a robber. The word used is 'lestes' in Greek, and could refer to a "robber, brigand, or insurrectionist" (Marsh pg600) and would often be used with reference to Zealots. Sanders and Mastin (pg399) suggest it is a word used as a "common description of nationalists given by an occupying power". It may be ironic to John, and the other gospel writers, that the Jews want an earthly bandit above a heavenly king. This characteristic feature of irony may be emphasisied here as the name Barabbas means 'son of the Father'.

Pilate then goes back to Jesus and has him scourged. While this would not be the right action against someone in whom there was 'no crime', it is possible that Pilate wishes to punish Jesus to this degree in the hope the Jews might accept it and then allow Jesus to go free. He wants to "appease the Jews" (Carson pg597) and so adopts a "fresh strategy to evoke sympathy" (Carson pg596). Jesus is also mocked as a king and struck by the soldiers. Brown (pg 886) notes that the scourging and mocking appear to be part of Pilate's benevolent plan for Jesus' release.

Pilate again returns to the Jews repeating that he still finds no crime in Jesus, and Jesus is brought out wearing the crown of thorns and scarlet robe (19v5) presented "as a beaten, harmless, and rather pathetic figure (Carson pg598). In true irony, Jesus is shown as a mocked king, though for the evangelist he is the true heavenly king. The irony continues as Pilate says, 'Behold the man.' Yet it should be noted that John wished to show Jesus as a human being (a feature throughout the Gospel) as well as the Logos come from above; Jesus is shown truly suffering as a human being.

The Chief Priests and officers lead the calls for Jesus' crucifixion, though Pilate tries for a third time to insist that he finds no crime in Jesus so if they want his crucifixion they are to take Jesus and do it themselves. Pilate is relinquishing responsibility and placing it onto the Jews. Yet if it is not legal for the Jews to execute a man, how can they crucify Jesus? Perhaps they know they cannot and that is why they tell Pilate Jesus must die as he has broken their law by making 'himself the Son of God'. To identify oneself as the Son of God or to claim messiahship did not of itself lead to the death penalty. It seems the Jews were of the opinion Jesus was making a direct claim to divinity, and so he was violating Jewish religious law (Grayston pg158), and using sonship to suggest he shared God's rights and authority (Carson pg599). John records that Jesus making himself Son of God made Pilate more afraid, suggesting he had already been in fear of Jesus, perhaps as he saw Jesus as a divine man. "The play upon his pagan superstition is nicely calculated." (Robinson pg264). However, the word 'more' may mean exceedingly (Sanders and Mastin pg401).

The interrogation of Jesus continues as Pilate re-enters the Praetorium taking Jesus with him. He, "the mouthpiece of the evangelist's theological inquiry" (Fortna pg171) asks Jesus where he is from (19v9), but Jesus does not immediately answer his question. This silence of Jesus is noted in the Synoptic Gospels and is generally linked to the Suffering Servant passage in Isaiah 53v7. Pilate points out he has the authority to release or execute Jesus, but Jesus responds that he only has power over Jesus because it has been granted to him from above; "it has been determined by God." (Bultmann pg662). Pilate may have earthly power but real absolute power comes from above. It may be Jesus "discerns the hand of God" (Carson pg600) in the events. Jesus also remarks that the one who delivered him had greater sin. There is no clear indication who Jesus meant, though Caiaphas or Judas are generally favoured (though note earlier comments about possibility of sympathetic treatment of Caiaphas, leading to a personal belief Judas is meant).

In 19v12 it is noted that Pilate tries to release Jesus but the Jews object; thus John is exonerating the Romans from the death of Jesus, and placing the guilt onto the Jews. This is "a tendency visible in early Christian literature" (Barrett pg542), as the Christian Church sought "tolerance from the Roman authorities" (Brown pg794). It is also seemingly a characteristic feature within the gospel as a whole. This means that Pilate has once more gone out to the Jews in another change of scene. The Jews then seem to trap Pilate, in some "psychological warfare against him" (Brown pg890), stating that if he releases Jesus who has made himself a king, he is no friend of Caesar. No doubt the Jews would be quick to report Pilate to the Emperor Tiberius. Carson (pg607) wonders if 'friend of Caesar' may have been an official title that had been earned by Pilate. Barrett (pg543) points out (though is not convinced by the argument) that another 'friend of Caesar' Sejanus had fallen out of favour in Rome in 31 AD. Pilate had connections with Sejanus so it would have been dangerous if Pilate was accused of acting against Tiberius' interests, particularly as Tiberius was pathologically suspicious.

So Jesus is brought out and Pilate sits (though some have suggested Jesus may be seated, and if so for 'irony', as for John, Jesus has a judgemental role) on the 'judgement seat'. The evangelist refers to the place as 'The Pavement' (19v13) stating it was Gabbatha in Hebrew. Grayston comments (pg158) "'The Pavement' (Greek lithostroton): paved with stones, possibly a tesselated or mosaic area. Nobody really knows what 'Gabbatha' meant. A paved area has been found in a building that may have been the Antonia, though possibly from a century later."

The evangelist indicates (19v14) it was the day of Preparation of the Passover (Nisan 14 according to the Jewish calendar) and was about noon. It is generally argued that the evangelist is pointing out that

Jesus was handed over and died on Preparation Day at the time when the Passover lambs were being prepared and slaughtered to suggest that Jesus himself becomes the Passover lamb, with all the symbolism involved in that image. This may be characteristic of John's presentation of Jesus. In contrast, according to the dating in the Synoptic Gospels, Jesus is executed on Nisan 15, the actual day of Passover.

Pilate has still not given Jesus to the Jews, and says to them 'Behold your king'. But they cry for Jesus' crucifixion; when Pilate asks, 'Shall I crucify your king?' it is the Chief Priests who respond that they have no king but Caesar. This response seems treachery both against God their king, and against the nationalism of Israel. Barrett (pg546) suggests the Jews thereby abdicated their own unique position of sovereignty under God, though Carson comments that it is part of apologetics of converting Jews to Christianity (pg606). Pilate finally yields to the will of the Jews and hands Jesus over to be crucified.

A summary of impressions of the trial before Pilate

- There is animosity between Pilate and the Jews.
- Pilate supports Jesus and wants to set him free, as Jesus is innocent.
- Jesus' kingship is discussed; he is no earthly king or political Messiah.
- The focus is on Jesus' control and his divine links, though he is also shown to be human.
- Though Pilate eventually hands Jesus over to be crucified, both he and the Romans seem exonerated from the responsibility for the death of Jesus; for the evangelist, the 'Jews' are to blame.
- Characteristic features – irony, kingship, Jesus' innocence, Jesus' divine and human links, Jewish opposition, and Jesus' sacrifice as the Passover Lamb.

▶THE CRUCIFIXION OF JESUS (19v17-37)

According to John's presentation, Jesus carries his own cross (though likely only the cross-beam) to Golgotha. In the Synoptic

Gospels, Simon of Cyrene, a character who does not occur in the Fourth Gospel, carries the cross. While there have been attempts to harmonise the different accounts, many suggest John's version of events has a deliberate theological motivation. The evangelist may have wanted Jesus to have no help in carrying the cross to suggest he alone was "effecting the redemption of the world" (Barrett pg548), and was the "sole master of his destiny" (Beasley-Murray pg345). It seems that John wished to present Jesus' control of events and his destiny as a characteristic feature.

John's omission of Simon of Cyrene may also be connected to the Gnostics, and particularly to Basilides. He argued that Jesus did not indeed die on the cross, but his place was taken by Simon of Cyrene. Carson (pg609) therefore suggests that "If that view were rising in John's Day (and there is no evidence it was), it is possible that John might find it expedient to omit mention of the Cyrene." Some argue (e.g. Barrett pg548, Smalley pg226) that a link may have been intended between Jesus carrying his cross to his death with that of Isaac, son of Abraham, carrying the wood on which he would be sacrificed (Genesis Chapter 22). If such a link was intended then in fact there would be contrast in the two incidents as Isaac was saved but Jesus goes on to die.

'Golgotha', 'the place of a skull', is a "site in doubt…. may have derived the name from appearance" (Carson pg609). Hence the modern attempts to find such a skull shaped place. John translates the Hebrew Golgotha, this may suggest that some of his target audience would be non-Jews. Jesus is crucified between two others (19v18). This may just be an historical detail, but it may also suggest Jesus' centrality in the unfolding events in which he has the importance, as (Beasley-Murray pg346) "the most honoured takes the place in the middle".

John records (19v19) that Pilate wrote and put on the cross a title, 'Jesus of Nazareth, the king of the Jews.' It is of course likely that he did not write the title himself, but John may be implying that Pilate may have seen some truth in what was written. In the Fourth Gospel this kingship of Jesus is both truth and a characteristic feature. The Jews object to what is written, as many Jews coming to Jerusalem for Passover read the words, written as they were in Hebrew, Latin and Greek. The different languages were respectively, "local, official, and commercial" (Grayston pg160), but they may also be suggestive that the evangelist is presenting Jesus' crucifixion as that of a universal saviour. The Jews want Pilate to write that Jesus merely claimed to be king of the Jews, and clearly his execution would show his claim was false. The Jews previously forced Pilate's hand with their comments that he was not 'Caesar's friend', but Pilate now stands firm refusing to pander to their wishes. His declaration 'What I have written, I have written', gives the last word to Pilate, his "act of revenge" (Carson pg610) against the taunting Jews.

Carson (pg608, 610) notes how Jesus may have been crucified. He may have been tied or nailed to the cross-member, which would then have been hoisted up and fastened to the vertical beam. His feet may have been placed on a footrest, the seducula, protruding from the vertical beam. Placing the feet on the footrest was not to relieve the agony but to actually increase it. This was because the crucified person would strain and push on the seducula so that his body would not collapse and be asphyxiated. The seducula prolonged the life, but also the agony, as the victim was encouraged to fight on.

The soldiers who crucify Jesus divide his garments between them; this was their right. However, John records that Jesus had a tunic that was woven in one piece. It has been noted (e.g. Marsh pg615) that this was similar to the tunic worn by the High Priest. John may be suggesting Jesus is the true High Priest who will offer himself on behalf of the people rather than make some animal sacrifice. Jesus' tunic may also be a symbol of the unity of the Church (Grayston pg161). The soldiers decide that rather than tearing and dividing the tunic they should cast lots for it. The evangelist notes that this in itself was to fulfil scripture (19v24), this time God's words, in Exodus 28v32 and Psalm 22v18. Carson correctly observes (pg612) that the fulfilment of scripture becomes more common, a characteristic feature, in the Fourth Gospel as we move into the Passion narratives. The soldiers then unknowingly take part in what is the plan of God himself.

John records (19v25) how certain women were standing by Jesus' cross, namely his mother Mary (previously mentioned in Chapter 2),

Mary the mother of Cleopas, and Mary Magdalene. Also standing there is the Beloved Disciple, "the sole representative of Jesus' associates" (Barrett pg552). The Beloved Disciple has been previously mentioned at the supper in Chapter 13, and possibly at 18v15 if the 'another disciple' mentioned there was the Beloved Disciple, but now within the closing narratives his treatment becomes a characteristic feature.

Jesus speaks to his mother and the disciple. He says to his mother, 'Woman, behold your son.', and to his disciple, 'Behold your mother.' Jesus seems to be replacing himself with the Beloved Disciple; he becomes the son. This may imply the evangelist's desire to establish the Beloved Disciple as the successor of Jesus, named as such by Jesus himself. The honour and importance of the Beloved Disciple would then be guaranteed. If the Beloved Disciple was none other than the evangelist himself (see 21v24) this would then strengthen the position of the Johannine Church and of the Fourth Gospel itself.

The Beloved Disciple is obedient and from that moment he is said to have taken 'her to his own home'. It may seem strange that Mary should go with the disciple as in Chapter 7 her other sons, who could look after her, are mentioned. However, in Chapter 7 the evangelist implies that there was some animosity of the brothers to Jesus. Perhaps the true family of Jesus, his supportive brothers, is the Church. If Jesus' 'woman' also relates Mary to Judaism, as Eve in Genesis 2v23 is 'Woman', then there would be in the new relationship of Mary and the Beloved Disciple the relationship of Judaism and the early Church (Marsh pg616). Bultmann suggests (pg673) that Mary represents Jewish Christianity and the Beloved Disciple represents Gentile Christianity.

In 19v28 John mentions how Jesus knew that 'all was now finished'. The 'knowingness' of Jesus is a characteristic feature in John's Gospel, and may be an attempt to suggest his prophetic ability or even more, his omniscience, thereby linking him with the divine. Jesus speaks again: this time he says, 'I thirst' which the evangelist records fulfilled scripture. The wording of John implies that the words are spoken deliberately for such fulfilment to occur. The 'I thirst' is linked with passages involving someone thirsty or parched, for example. Psalm 69v3, v21 and Psalm 22v15 are cited. Both these Psalms end on a note of triumph, which may be in the evangelist's mind at this point. Jesus may mean physical thirsting, in which case there is a glimpse of his true humanity, or he may be thirsting for God as he now completes his tasks.

A sponge full of vinegar is placed on a hyssop and held to his mouth (18v29). Barrett (pg 553) notes that hyssop is "important in Passover observance", used as it is to spread the protective power of Passover blood (Grayston pg163). This may be significant to John as he is thought to present, as a characteristic feature, Jesus as the Passover Lamb. However, Grayston prefers a link of hyssop with cleansing, citing Psalm 51v7, and in particular with cleansing of outcasts of society. John the evangelist may have one or both these links in mind and uses hyssop thereby to make theological statements about Jesus. Some point out (e.g. Barrett pg553) that hyssop might be suitable for sprinkling but not presenting a wet sponge as it lacks the stiffness required. Carson (pg620) refers to the possibility that the original word used was in fact 'hysso' which is a javelin.

Jesus receives the vinegar and says, 'It is finished.' (19v30); this may mean that Jesus' suffering is over, though the suffering of Jesus on the cross has not been emphasised by the evangelist. Carson (pg621) notes that the verb used for 'finished' means "carrying out of a task….fulfilling one's religious obligations." Jesus may see the task of God completed, and "dies as the one who completes his earthly work, who carries out the Father's commission obediently to the end." (Schnackenburg pg284). Jesus has been lifted up to glory, and the cross is thus a victorious event.

Jesus' words on the cross in John seem "composed and confident" (Grayston pg163), and in contrast to his apparent despair in Mark's Gospel. So Jesus 'bowed his head and gave up his spirit', signifying "his readiness" (Brown pg930) to die. The evangelist may be suggesting that Jesus' life was not in reality taken from him, rather he himself, characteristically in control, "makes a conscious act – a self offering" (Beasley-Murray pg353) and gives up his life. The bowing of the head may have prevented breathing and caused Jesus' death.

In 19v31 the evangelist again reminds the reader that these events all took place on the day of Preparation, Nisan 14, and records how the Jews are eager that the bodies of those crucified should not remain on the cross into the next day, Nisan 15. This was 'a high day' and also the 'sabbath'. To hasten death by inducing asphyxia the Jews ask Pilate that their legs may be broken. The legs of the two criminals crucified with Jesus are broken (probably smashed with a mallet – Carson pg672) by the soldiers, but when they come to Jesus they 'saw that he was already dead' and so 'they did not break his legs' (19v33).

Jesus had died very quickly by crucifixion standards, and (Marsh pg620) "too soon for normal expectation." This may have led to suggestions that Jesus had not in fact died on the cross, particularly as his legs were not broken. The evangelist states he 'was already dead', and to show that this was indeed true he records (19v34) that the soldiers actually to make sure he was dead pierced his side with a spear, 'and at once there came out blood and water'. The physiological possibility of this happening is generally discussed (e.g. Barrett pg556; Carson pg623), but more concern is often given to the purpose of the evangelist in his account.

Generally scholars suggest (as above) the evangelist wished to show that Jesus was a real man who really died (Barrett pg556) a real death (Sanders and Mastin pg411), as Jesus was "physical in the fullest sense" (Marsh pg622). The evangelist may also have wanted to combat docetic ideas that Jesus did not really die as he was not a real man but 'appeared' to be human. The same scholars also consider how the blood and water in particular might also by symbols. Barrett (pg556) suggests the historical also conveys theological truth, and Sanders and Mastin (pg411) couples the real death with featured symbolism. The Eucharistic link with the blood and water seems a strong possibility (though Carson, pg624, also considers the flow indicating life and cleansing). If the blood and water are symbols of the Eucharist then John may be suggesting the rite is thus "sanctioned and empowered" (Carson pg624).

It is also possible that the 'water' may be a veiled symbol for baptism; if so, the evangelist by reference to both Eucharist and baptism, would be emphasising the importance of the sacraments. However, the water may refer to the giving of the spirit. The evangelist stated in Chapter 7v38-39 that living waters would flow 'out of his heart', and he indicated this referred to the Spirit, with the implication this would be given when Jesus was glorified. This would be appropriate within the crucifixion story, as the crucifixion is itself that moment when Jesus is indeed glorified.

To further stress the truth of his 'evidence' the evangelist mentions (19v35) that the events described were seen, characteristically, by a witness, and that 'his testimony is true'. The hope is 'that you also may believe'. This witness may be the Beloved Disciple and apparent author of the gospel (21v24), which would give reliability both to the events, and the Gospel's record itself. Indeed Barrett (pg 58) considers the indication of the truthful witness may even be a later addition to secure authority for the gospel.

Even further support for the historicity of events is given when the evangelist states that 'these things took place that scripture might be fulfilled', something which seems emphasised in the Passion narrative. For John, this means that these events are all in God's hands and have his authority behind them. Fortna (p178) suggests that this fulfilment of prophecy is "the heart of the passion narratives' rationale." John first refers to 'not a bone of him shall be broken' for which there are scripture links in Exodus 12v46, Numbers 9v12, and Psalm 34v20. The second reference 'They shall look on him whom they have pierced' is linked to Zechariah 12v10.

A summary of impressions of the crucifixion of Jesus

- A quiet, well ordered scene, with Jesus in control (Grayston pg160) – contrast with Mark's account as in John there is no emphasis on Jesus' agony, no mockery while on the cross, and no cry of dereliction (Sanders and Mastin pg 410).
- Jesus is presented as universal king.
- There is fulfilment of various scriptures.
- The words of Jesus from the cross in the Fourth Gospel are unique to that gospel.
- The Beloved Disciple is present and immediately obeys Jesus.

- Jesus is shown to be definitely dead.
- There may be links to the sacraments of baptism and Eucharist.
- Characteristic features – Jesus in control, his kingship, scriptural fulfilment, the Beloved Disciple, Jesus knowingness, sacramental material, and witness and belief.

▶ THE BURIAL OF JESUS (19v38-42)

In his presentation of the burial of Jesus, John mentions, as do the Synoptic Gospel writers, Joseph of Arimathea. Arimathea was a city in the province of Judaea, which Marsh notes (pg623) was 60 miles from Jerusalem and 13 miles ENE of Lydda.

John states that Joseph was a disciple of Jesus but not openly 'for fear of the Jews'. Here would appear to be what Brown in his 'The Gospel according to John' names as a 'crypto-Christian', as he keeps it secret that he is a disciple of Jesus. Yet Joseph bravely, given the recent circumstances, goes to Pilate and requests that he might take away the body of Jesus. He is allowed to do so, but peculiarly to John he is accompanied by Nicodemus. John reminds the reader (19v39) that this was the Nicodemus 'who had at first come to him by night' (in Chapter 3).

The association of Nicodemus at this point with Joseph, identified as a disciple of Jesus, may lead to the belief that Nicodemus was also himself a disciple, and also a secret one (Robinson pg284). In Chapter 3 John may have presented Nicodemus as symbolically in the dark, though at least willing to come to Jesus to seek answers to his questions. In Chapter 7v51 Nicodemus had seemingly defended Jesus' right to be heard by the Sanhedrin, of which Nicodemus was a member, before they made judgements about him. John may intend in Chapter 19 to suggest that Nicodemus has now become convinced enough about Jesus to become his disciple. Carson (pg629) states that Nicodemus now steps out of the darkness into the light, while Beasley-Murray (pg359 – quoting Hoskyns) remarks that Nicodemus and Joseph, "two timorous believers are publicly and courageously drawn to the Christ after his exaltation on the cross.", thereby fulfilling the required role of discipleship.

The pair bring with them 'a mixture of myrrh and aloes about a hundred pounds weight', which Marsh (pg623) notes was the normal means of preparing a body for burial, but that the amount was "lavish". Carson (pg630) comments that the mixture was not actually to embalm the body but to give fragrance and stifle the smell of putrefaction. Bandages would have been wound around the body with the spices spread between layers, as John comments 'is the burial custom of the Jews' (19v40). This comment seems to imply that the reader may not have been Jewish and aware of this 'custom'. The action and the amount of aloes may show the love that Joseph and Nicodemus had for Jesus, and were "probably intended as an indication of the devotion of these loyal followers of Jesus." (Fortna pg180). John may also be suggesting that Jesus' burial was a "royal burial" (Brown pg960).

In 19v42 John again informs the reader that these events happened on the Day of Preparation. He also indicates that in the place where Jesus was crucified there was a garden, which Marsh (pg623) suggests from the language suggests a sizeable plot; perhaps an orchard or plantation, and which (Carson pg 631) is sizeable enough to prepare us for the gardener in Chapter 20. In the garden there was a tomb. His comment that the tomb was 'new where no one had ever been laid' may have been to prepare for the later resurrection and the point that only one body was resurrected, namely that of Jesus (Carson pg631). The Synoptic Gospels record that the tomb was that of Joseph, though John is silent on that point.

A summary of impressions of the burial of Jesus

- Both Joseph and Nicodemus may have been disciples of Jesus. They were influential and important members of the Jews, and may be used (Sanders and Mastin pg414) to support the historicity of the statement made by John in 12v42, that many rulers believed in Jesus, but would not confess it as they would then be excluded from the synagogue.
- Jesus is buried according to Jewish custom.
- The burial again suggests that Jesus was actually dead.
- Characteristic features – discipleship, and the humanity of Jesus who has died and is now buried.

THE RESURRECTION NARRATIVES:

▶THE EMPTY TOMB (Chapter 20v1-10)

Mary Magdalene (she was from Magdala) visits the tomb while it is still dark, in contrast to Mark's 'when the sun had risen' (16v2), and sees the stone, not previously mentioned in John, has been rolled away. It is possible the 'dark' is symbolic, perhaps of Mary's lack of appreciation for while she is aware of the physical removal of the stone she fails to realise that Jesus has risen. Carson comments (pg635) that the "darkness of the hour is the perfect counterpart to the darkness that shrouds Mary's understanding."

She runs to tell Simon Peter and the Beloved Disciple. The evangelist does not state that Mary has looked in the tomb, nor at this point in the Johannine story has seen angels, but she believes that Jesus' body has been taken and laid elsewhere. She states (v2) 'They have taken the Lord out of the tomb, and we do not know where they have laid him.', though the 'they' is unspecific. The 'we' mentioned by Mary hints there may be other women with her as per the synoptic tradition; John may wish to concentrate on Mary alone.

The Beloved Disciple is peculiar to John's Gospel. Both disciples run together but the evangelist informs us that the Beloved Disciple outran Peter arriving at the tomb first. The Beloved Disciple looks into the tomb but does not enter, while Peter goes straight in, "with characteristic impetuosity" (Bruce pg385). Scholars debate whether the evangelist may be indicating some superiority of the Beloved Disciple over Peter in his narrative. For example, the evangelist repeats the point that the Beloved Disciple arrived at the tomb first. Also it is the impetuous Peter who rushes into the tomb, while the Beloved Disciple hesitates, possibly to demonstrate the respect that should be shown to Jesus. This also contrasts with Luke 24v12 (only present in certain manuscripts) that Peter went to the tomb, stooped to look in, but then returned home 'wondering'. Moreover it is the Beloved Disciple who, characteristicaly, is said to see and believe; this is not said of Peter, who may be "'beholding' the discarded grave-clothes without believing (Strachan, pg324), "puzzled by what he saw." (Bruce pg385). Barrett notes (pg 563) that as Peter 'followed' the Beloved disciple, and following in John is usually significant, it may be intended to "subordinate Peter to the Beloved Disciple". Yet Barrett also comments that "we must however be careful not to suggest that John identified fleetness of foot with apostolic pre-eminence."; while Brown (pg1005) argues that the "writer's purpose is not to detract from Peter but to exalt the status of the beloved Disciple."

Beasley-Murray (pg373) notes that "It is fashionable to talk about the 'rivalry' existing between Peter and the Beloved Disciple, and between the churches that adhered to them", with 20:3-10 regarded as "an attempt to play down that rivalry". However, while he feels there is no depreciation of Peter, he still comments that "Peter is not the hero of the Fourth Gospel, the Beloved Disciple has that role." Yet the evangelist states (v9) that 'as yet they did not know the scripture, that he must rise from the dead', perhaps there has not been perfect appreciation even on the part of the 'ideal' Beloved Disciple up to this point. Though if the Beloved Disciple is the evangelist he is himself "confessing the paucity of his understanding of scripture at this point." Various scholars suggest the particular scripture, Psalm 16v10, may be in the evangelist's mind.

The separation of the napkin and linen cloths noted in (v7) may be intended to suggest that Jesus had risen from his grave clothes, "passed through the cloths" (Barrett pg563), "emerged from his burial wrappings" (Brown pg1007), rather than have merely been unbound. This detail may also be apologetic material to defend the resurrection from those who suggested the body must have been stolen from the tomb. Thieves would not "have been likely to leave behind expensive linen and even more expensive spices." (Carson pg637). However, there is not total agreement among scholars about the positioning of the grave clothes.

The mention of the two disciples returning 'home' poses the problem of where the disciples lived. Peter was a fisherman from Galilee. Similarly, if the traditional identification of the Beloved Disciple with John son of Zebedee is correct, he was also a fisherman from Galilee. Is the evangelist suggesting that they also had homes in the vicinity of Jerusalem? If the Beloved Disciple is not the fisherman he could of course be from the south.

A summary of impressions of the Empty Tomb
- It is established that Jesus has risen from the dead.
- He has risen from the grave clothes.
- The evangelist may be suggesting some superiority of the Beloved Disciple over Peter.
- Characteristic features – light and darkness, symbolism, the Beloved Disciple and Peter, discipleship, and seeing and believing.

THE APPEARANCE TO MARY MAGDALENE (Chapter 20v11-18)

This section centres on Mary and her meeting with the resurrected Jesus. It may be significant that "the first reunion is with an individual, a woman, who according to the tradition of the church held no position of authority within it." (Lightfoot pg330). She initially stands at the tomb weeping, and then peers into the tomb seeing two angels. The presence of angels may "witness that the powers of heaven have been at work." (Beasley-Murray p373). Marsh notes (pg635) that angels were introduced into Jewish theology under Persian influence and offered to austere Jewish monotheism a way to establish Yahweh's communication with people on earth. The evangelist mentions they are where the body had lain, thereby re-indicating that Jesus has risen.

Mary is asked by the angels and by Jesus why she weeps, perhaps not for information but as a "gentle reproof" (Carson pg640). There is no indication in the text that she appreciates the two in the tomb to be angels, and she believes Jesus to be the gardener. Brown (pg1009) considers that the identification by Mary of Jesus with the gardener may "be an acted-out form of Johannine misunderstanding". It seems strange that Mary fails to recognise Jesus though she is weeping and the tears may blur her vision. The two people on the road to Emmaus (Luke 24) also fail initially to recognise it is Jesus who has joined them on their journey. This raises questions about the nature of the resurrected Jesus; in particular as to whether he has changed in appearance.

Mary shows her love for her Lord in asking where his body has been laid so she can remove it. When Jesus calls her by name she realises it is Jesus and refers to him as Rabboni, which John translates "for his Greek speaking readers" (Carson pg641) as 'Master', probably in his role as teacher. 'Rabboni' may be a little more affectionate than 'rabbi', "more personally expressed" (Schnackenburg pg317).

Jesus instructs her not to touch him, as he has to ascend to the Father. It is possible she merely appeared likely to touch him or was already touching him; if the latter is the case, and Marsh (pg637) indicates the Greek suggests "cease from clinging to me", then Jesus is physically resurrected. Later (v27) Jesus invites Thomas to actually touch him, which is in direct contrast to his words to Mary. This has led to debate as to whether the evangelist believed Jesus ascended to the Father after he had appeared to Mary and then returned from heaven to later appear to his disciples and Thomas. The passage emphasises the authority of Jesus in ascending, and his relationship with 'my Father' (v17). He instructs Mary to tell the disciples that this is to happen. Mary obeys and tells them that she has 'seen the Lord' (v18), thereby acting as a witness to the resurrection of Jesus.

A summary of impressions of the appearance to Mary Magdalene

- A woman is the first to see the resurrected Jesus.
- There may be a possibility that the appearance of the resurrected Jesus is different from that seen before.
- Jesus is to ascend to his Father.
- Mary acts as a witness of Jesus' resurrection
- Characteristic features – importance of women, lack of understanding and appreciation, and witness.

▶ **THE FIRST APPEARANCE TO THE DISCIPLES (Chapter 20v19-23)**

That same evening, Sunday the first day of the week, the disciples were assembled in a room; its doors were shut, as they were afraid of the Jews. They may have felt their lives were in danger after the recent events, though the evangelist could be presenting symbolically the Christian community under threat of persecution.

Jesus appears in the midst of the disciples. This again raises questions about the nature of the resurrected Jesus, as it appears he passes "through solid matter" (Barrett pg567) or just materialises within the room rather than entering through the door, as it was locked.

Jesus offers his 'peace' to them in their troubled state; this is presumably a religious and inner peace that will aid and reassure them. He also shows them his hands and side; the evangelist may be stressing it was definitely Jesus who was before them, the nail and spear marks would be proof of this. The disciples are glad to see Jesus, and he gives them their commission. He is the sent one of God, now they in turn are sent as apostles.

Jesus breathes on them the Holy Spirit. This is reminiscent of God breathing life into Adam in Genesis; John may here intend to show Jesus' connection with God even to the extent of implying his divinity. Jesus also seems empowered to pass on to the disciples the Holy Spirit, again seemingly a divine act. The word used for the Holy Spirit here is 'Pneuma' rather than the 'Paracletos' (Paraclete) of the farewell discourses. Scholars debate how this giving (on the first Sunday) of the Holy Spirit fits in with Luke's account in the Acts of the Apostles (Chapter 2) of the Holy Spirit descending much later at Pentecost. Suggestions (e.g. Carson pg649ff) include John is presenting an acted parable or a symbolic breathing, pointing forward to the full giving of the Spirit at Pentecost.

The passage ends with the indication of the authority of the disciples, and perhaps for the evangelist, the "pardoning authority of the church" (Marsh pg643). According to John's presentation the disciples are granted the power to forgive or retain the sins of people. Beasley-Murray (pg383) suggests that the language implies a judge's declaration of guilt or innocence, which as a Johannine characteristic, and in the Christian sense, is judgement and salvation.

A summary of impressions of the first appearance to the disciples

- Jesus appears to be able to materialise and de-materialise, or pass through solid objects.
- Jesus gives the disciples their commission – they are sent as he has been, and are given authority to act in judgement.
- The peace of Jesus and the Holy Spirit are given to the disciples (the church?).

- Characteristic features – symbolism, Holy Spirit, salvation and judgement, and the divine links of Jesus.

▶ THE DOUBT OF THOMAS (Chapter 20v24-25)

The appearance of Jesus has not been witnessed by the disciple Thomas; he refuses to believe the report of the disciples that they have seen the risen 'Lord' showing (Marsh pg645) "understandable scepticism and pardonable candour". Yet this is the same disciple who in Chapter 11v16 had bravely stated that he and the other disciples should go with Jesus to Jerusalem so 'that we may die with him.' Thomas needs visual and physical proof, "empirical evidence" (Fortna pg194) before he will believe; he needs to see and touch the marks of the nails and thrust his hand into Jesus' side, presumably into the place where the spear had pierced Jesus' side when he was crucified. Thomas may be used by the evangelist to represent all those who need physical proof, a "type of those who demand tangible proofs and precise definitions of what they are expected to believe as Christians." ('The Fourth Gospel', Strachan pg330).

'Believing' is an area emphasised by the evangelist throughout his gospel, and Thomas has not managed to show the believing necessary, though the Beloved Disciple, Mary, and the other disciples have done so. Yet it should be noted that all the gospels have the feature of doubt of the resurrection. Dodd (Tradition, pg145) sees in this incident, in the evangelist's own style, "a dramatization of the traditional motive of the incredulity of some or all of the disciples."

A summary of impressions of the doubt of Thomas

- Thomas does not believe the witness of his fellow disciples that Jesus has risen.
- Thomas requires evidence before he will believe – namely to see and touch Jesus.
- Characteristic features – believing and non-believing.

▶ THE SECOND APPEARANCE TO THE DISCIPLES (Chapter 20v26-29)

The evangelist begins the section with 'Eight days later'. As the Jews count the present day as day 1, (inclusive reckoning), this means that the event again falls on the Sunday, a week after the first appearance of Jesus to the disciples. It may be that the Sunday, the first day of the week is being established as the 'Lord's Day', the Christian day of worship, celebrating the day Jesus rose from the dead. This may be a "subtle allusion to the origins of Christian worship on this particular day." (Carson pg657).

The 'he said to Thomas' of v27, seems to suggest that Jesus may have come specifically to reveal himself to Thomas, perhaps "to put right once and for all the issue as between sight…and belief." (Marsh pg648). The disciples, this time including Thomas, are assembled again in a room with the doors shut. There is no mention now of their fear, though Jesus still greets them with his peace. Again Jesus seems to have 'appeared' within the room. He invites the doubting Thomas to touch him, to not be faithless but believing. It is not clear whether Thomas needs to physically touch Jesus to bring him to belief; however, the invitation seems to suggest the evangelist himself believed Jesus to be physically present, possessing a real body.

Thomas, his "resolute scepticism vanished" (Bruce pg394), makes a great pronouncement of faith as he acknowledges Jesus as both Lord and God. 'Lord', in Greek 'kurios', seems an early Christian post-resurrection title. Carson suggests (pg658) that as kurios is used in the LXX (the Greek translation of the Hebrew Old Testament) of God himself, then in many occurrences it is to be consider on the same level as 'theos' ('God'). John's coupling of 'kurios' and 'theos' here in respect of Jesus, clearly stresses Jesus' authority, and may suggest his divinity. Indeed, the two words were used by the Emperor Domitian to claim divinity for himself. Thomas' acknowledgement seems a "personal confession of faith" (Carson pg6590) as he uses the pronoun 'my' (Lord and God). It may be that John's selection of material is also to bring the reader to a similar confession. Yet Thomas does not receive praise; indeed Jesus, perhaps in veiled criticism of his previous unbelief, comments that Thomas has only believed because he has seen the risen Jesus, while he praises those future believers who without such 'proof' come themselves to faith.

A summary of impressions of the second appearance to the disciples

- Sunday may be established as the Lord's Day and the day of Christian worship.
- Proof is given to Thomas that Jesus has truly risen.
- Thomas makes a great confession of faith – that Jesus is his Lord and his God.
- Characteristic features – believing, Jesus' divine and also human links.

▶CLOSING VERSES (Chapter 20v30-31)

The writer indicates that Jesus performed many other signs before his disciples, which are not included in the gospel, though he has recorded a number of Jesus' signs. This indicates that the writer is aware of others but that he has made a selection for inclusion, presumably because they were particular appropriate to further his message. The Greek word for signs is 'semeia' which suggests the evangelist wishes to indicate the actions of Jesus are to be seen as signposting people towards John's particular good news. That good news seems indicated in v31. It is that life can be obtained through Jesus' name.

However, in order to receive that prize, it is necessary for people to believe, a feature examined throughout the Gospel; to bring about (or 'confirm' – see below) that belief is the purpose of the evangelist's record of Jesus' signs, or possibly the whole of his gospel material. The evangelist indicates what it is that must be believed. He states belief is necessary in Jesus as the Christ, the Messiah. Also Jesus is to be believed in as the Son of God. In the various manuscripts of John's Gospel two different Greek words are used for the 'believing' mentioned at this point. One Greek word is 'pisteuete' (the present subjunctive) which suggests continuing to hold the faith, whereas the other Greek word 'pisteusete' (the aorist subjunctive) indicates "making an act of faith" (Beasley-Murray pg387) from previous non-belief. The variant words raise the question as to the evangelist's purpose in writing the gospel. The former ('pisteuete') implies the material is written to aid the faith of those already believing, while the later ('pisteusete') would suggest the intention is to convert non-believers to faith, to act as "a missionary tract to convert the Hellenistic world." (Barrett pg575).

This final verse (v31) of Chapter 20 has been suggested as being John's signing off comment. Clearly it would be an appropriate place for the gospel to end. However, there is a further chapter.

A summary of impressions of the closing verses of Chapter 20

- Only some of Jesus' signs have been recorded.

- The purpose of signs (and possible of the other words and actions recorded in the gospel) is so that readers may believe Jesus is the Messiah and Son of God thereby obtaining life.

- Characteristic features – signs, believing, and Jesus' divine links.

▶ THE APPEARANCE OF JESUS BY THE SEA OF GALILEE (Chapter 21vv1-25)

There is considerable debate among scholars as to whether or not Chapter 21 was original to the gospel, particularly in view of the apparent 'signing off' by the evangelist in 20v30-31. Carson (pg665) suggests that "Most contemporary interpreters have concluded that John 21 was not part of the Fourth Gospel as it was first written, and that assuming John 21 was added later, it was added by someone other than the evangelist." It has been noted (e.g. Marsh pg653) that there are 28 Greek words in chapter 21 that are not elsewhere in the gospel, and that there are differences in linguistic style.

Yet scholars (e.g. again Marsh pg654) also generally point to the possible support for Chapter 21 being by the same author as Chapters 1-20. It may have been "composed with the rest of the gospel" (Carson pg665) or added later by the evangelist in "some sort of hurried editorial work" (Marsh pg654). In support it is noted that there are also similarities of speech, themes and purposes within Chapter 21 that are found elsewhere in the gospel. Some (e.g. Streeter, quoted by Strachan pg333) suggest that if Chapter 21 is an addition it "must have been written early" and possibly by a pupil of the author but one "saturated in his master's spirit."

Chapter 21 is referred to in a number of different ways. For example as an 'appendix' (Barrett pg 576), or 'epilogue' (Carson pg665), or a 'supplement (Strachan 333). Beasley-Murray (pg 395) also offers "In the estimate of the majority of New Testament scholars chapter 21 is an addendum to the gospel, whether it be described as an appendix, a postscript, or an epilogue."

v1-3. The evangelist records that Jesus showed himself by the Sea of Galilee to his disciples in the following incident. Seven disciples were together, namely Simon Peter, Thomas, Nathanael, the sons of Zebedee (i.e. James and John), and two others. One of these seven disciples is the Beloved Disciple but it is not possible to identify him from using the list because of the two unnamed disciples. Indeed Beasley-Murray seems to imply (pg 398) that the extra two are added in order to make the identification of the Beloved Disciple impossible so keeping the identity secret.

It may be significant that seven disciples are mentioned. The number seven was consider the 'perfect' number; so possibly the group of disciples are symbols of the perfect disciples or church. Yet Marsh (pg661) considers that "the number 7 is not likely to be meant as the 'perfect' number".

Peter announces he is going fishing. This may indicate a turning back to his old trade rather than going out and fulfilling the required mission Jesus had indicated in 20v21. Marsh argues (pg658) that for Peter to say he is going fishing "is really to say, 'The whole episode of our discipleship, our following of Jesus of Nazareth is over. We had better go back to our fishing.'" Peter may have gone 'physically' fishing rather than becoming a fisher of men. Moreover, he is the one who may thereby tempt his fellow disciples to turn back to their previous duties. However, if there is veiled criticism of Peter, then it is to be shared by the other disciples, including the supposedly 'ideal' Beloved Disciple, who willingly go with him. Marsh points out (pg669) that even if Peter and the others are not committing apostasy against Jesus and the Father, nor tuning back to fishing because of despair, "the fishing expedition and the dialogue that ensues do not read like the lives of men on a Spirit-empowered mission."

It is perhaps not surprising that they fail to catch anything. They have been fishing at night, which in fishing terms "was the best time for fishing" (Marsh pg662). However, this means that they were trying to catch fish while it was dark; this for the evangelist is symbolic of evil and apostasy, and also of unenlightenment, a time without the 'light of the world' Jesus.

v4-8. Jesus stands on the beach, and appropriately in the light, as it is now morning, 'day was breaking'. The disciples are not initially aware that the person is Jesus. Again questions are raised about the resurrected person of Jesus and why he is not immediately recognisable. He addresses them affectionately as 'children' and asks if they have caught anything. On being told 'no' he instructs them to cast the net on the right side of the boat. They obey and in consequence catch so many fish that they cannot drag it into the boat. The evangelist's message may simply be that to achieve anything, the disciples, and whatever they may represent, need Jesus to aid them and with his aid the results will be 'miraculous'. There is the possibility of symbolism within the incident, namely that the net is representative of the church drawing in many converts. If this is the case then the suggestion is for the disciples to concentrate on their spiritual commission not on their earthly thoughts and concerns. The incident may be thus be a 'sign', though it may not be a miracle, as Jesus could merely have noticed a shoal of fish from his advantage point.

The Beloved Disciple is the one (v7) who recognises Jesus, whom he acknowledges, is 'the Lord'. Peter hears it is Jesus from the Beloved Disciple and puts on his fisher's coat. The text states he had been naked, but he may have been wearing a loincloth. Perhaps Peter feels it necessary to be dressed to come into Jesus' presence. He then eagerly, and perhaps as usual, impetuously jumps into the sea. "Characteristically the Beloved Disciple exhibits quick insight, and Peter quick action." (Carson pg671).

The other disciples remain in the boat dragging the catch of fish to the shore, 'about a hundred yards'. While Peter's eagerness to be with Jesus may be commendable, the evangelist may intend his action to be viewed carefully and possibly symbolically. It may be that Peter's nakedness is representative of his "spiritual state" (Brown pg1096), possibly of his sin, which he tries to hide from Jesus. Or it may be he is on the first stage of some recovery and has taken up his role of disciple again. At times within his gospel John when mentioning water may be alluding to baptism; this may be the case here. Now it is Peter who needs washing clean, and he plunges headlong to that requirement. It is significant that no one else jumps into the sea, for he has separated himself from the others in the boat, (the church ?) who bring the fish to the shore.

v9-14. When they all arrive at the shore there is a charcoal fire there, and on it fish and bread. Previously when such a fire was mentioned Peter was sharing its warmth in the court of the High Priest, standing with those responsible for Jesus' arrest. Is Peter now being offered the opportunity to move from the enemy fold into the fold of his true shepherd? It has been suggested that in Chapter 6, where bread and fish were mentioned, the evangelist may have been concerned with Eucharistic teaching; the same suggestion is therefore possible here. Barrett states (pg578) that the meal "has evidently some eucharistic significance", while Bultmann (pg710) suggests it is "a replica of the Lord's Supper." Marsh notes (pg666) that in Christian art the bread of the sacrament is accompanied by fish and not wine. So are the disciples to share in morning communion with their risen Lord? They are invited by Jesus to come and eat, just as future converts may be invited within the later Eucharistic service. Jesus takes the bread, now mentioned first, and the fish, and gives them to the disciples. It may be implied that they have to contribute to the meal by bringing some of their catch. Though the bringing fish to Jesus may rather be symbolic of bringing potential followers to Jesus.

It is Peter who commendably responds and goes to drag the net full of great fish to the shore. Apparently there were 153 fish in the net, and as stated they were 'great'. It seems unlikely that the fish would have been counted, or that it is merely a randomly chosen number merely to suggest a lot. Perhaps the number is representative of something that the evangelist wishes to convey, though Carson notes (pg673) that "if the evangelist has some symbolism in mind connected with the number 153, he has hidden it well." Generally accepted is the view expressed by Marsh (pg665) that it may have been accepted that there were 153 species of fish and so the number represents a universal church, and the catch "parabolic of the successful universal mission of the church". Other suggestions would include 153 representing important churches, or even important individuals, perhaps within the Johannine community. St. Augustine offered a mathematical explanation; he noted that if the numbers 1 to 17 were added together, the result would be 153.

It should also be noted that the net is able to contain the fish without being broken. If symbolism is intended it may be that unity of the community is being indicated, the net "a picture of the undivided church" ('St. John's Gospel', Lightfoot pg340). Yet it may be that such unity, which the evangelist feels necessary to be indicated, was not at the time of the evangelist the actual situation.

In v12 the evangelist writes, 'none of the disciples dared ask him, "Who are you?" They knew it was the Lord.' This comment again raises questions. While the evangelist affirms it was Jesus their Lord, the implication seems to be that the person that they were actually seeing before them might not have the same physical appearance they had previously seen. The evangelist may have considered that if the disciples had asked if it was Jesus then this would have meant that they might doubt it was, and also serve to fuel the opinion of those who doubted or attacked the suggestion that Jesus was resurrected. The evangelist points out in v14 that this was the third time Jesus appeared to the disciples. This fits in with the material in Chapter 20, for while this is the fourth resurrection appearance, one of the previous ones had been to Mary Magdalene.

v15-19. These verses concentrate on dialogue between Jesus and Peter. Verse 15 opens with the statement 'when they had dined', which implies that Peter had shared in the breakfast meal. Jesus addresses Simon Peter as son of John (in Revised Standard Version) or Jonas. It may be that this is merely a historical indication, though if Jonas/Jonah was intended and it is symbolic, it may be the evangelist wishes to draw connections with Jonah in the Old Testament. Both Peter and Jonah went into the sea as both were wishing to pursue a course of action that was not that required. Both eventually emerged from the waters, and in the case of Jonah from the whale, to be challenged to do as was required.

So here in the gospel, Jesus asks Peter if he loves Jesus 'more than these'. This is a little ambiguous as it could mean more than Peter loves people or things, or that Peter loves Jesus "more than these others do" (Bruce pg404). Peter replies positively, and is given a pastoral commission to 'Feed my lambs'. Jesus asks the question a second time, and when Peter responds again in the affirmative, Jesus tells him to 'Tend my sheep.' The third questioning of Peter's love grieved Peter, presumably because it was seen by the disciple to recall his threefold denial of Jesus. Yet the denial of Jesus "was a profoundly serious failure, which called for a process of re-establishment commensurate with the seriousness of the defection." (Beasley-Murray pg405). Peter again states he loves Jesus and is this time told to 'Feed my sheep.'

It would appear that this threefold protestation of love means that in some way Peter has attempted to make up for his denial of Jesus, effecting a "rehabilitation to discipleship after his fall (Brown pg1111). Indeed, Jesus in giving Peter work to accomplish, as it appears in tending to the needs of Christians, whether new (lambs) to the faith or 'sheep' of the community, appears to bring Peter back into the fold. Thus Peter through the "devastating experience of fall" has enjoyed "restoration to the fellowship of his Lord." (Beasley-Murray pg707). Moreover, v18-19 indicates Jesus' awareness of the destiny of Peter in martyrdom, and in dying for the glory of God, for Peter's re-instatement was "to service' (Carson pg679) as "guardian of his master's flock" ('St. John's Gospel' Lightfoot pg340).

While it may not be significant, as some argue, (e.g. Barrett pg584, Lightfoot pg343), it should be noted that 'love' in the conversation between Peter and Jesus is indicated by two different Greek words. Initially Jesus asks Peter, 'Do you agapas me Peter?', to which Peter replies, 'You know I philo you'. Jesus repeats again using the verb agape, and again Peter replies using the verb philo. The third time Jesus also uses the verb philo as 'phileis' and Peter again states 'I philo you'. The Greek philo means to love as a friend, whereas agape, "the distinctively Christian word for love" (Marsh pg669), denotes a deeper love, a steadfast love that is required of true lovers of God. Hence it is possible that when called upon by Jesus to show this depth of love Peter can only offer the more superficial love of friendship, which Jesus seems to accept by using philo himself in the third question. Peter may have made up for his denial yet it appears he has not managed to progress to the point desired by Jesus. However, it is clear from Jesus' words in v18 that he knows eventually Peter will show a love that leads to his own death; Jesus "does not wait upon a man's attainment of perfection" (Marsh pg670) and so invites Peter to follow him. This suggests that Peter, because of his previous failure, needs to be re-invited by Jesus to respond and perform the discipleship necessary.

v20-23. Peter, instead of doing as asked, turns around. He sees the Beloved Disciple who, as might be expected, is already following. The evangelist reminds us that the Beloved Disciple had been the one who asked Jesus at the supper who should betray him. Peter asks Jesus what is to be the fate of the Beloved Disciple. Jesus states 'If it is my will that he remains until I come, what is that to you? Follow me.' Jesus is seemingly telling Peter to mind his own business and do what he has been told to do, namely follow Jesus. Lightfoot (pg342) considers Jesus' statement "certainly contains a rebuke of Peter."

The evangelist then refers to how the brethren believed Jesus had indicated that the Beloved Disciple would not die, taking 'remains' to mean 'remains alive'. Yet the evangelist seems keen to show, by repeating Jesus' words, that that is not what Jesus had actually said. The reason for this material may be because the Beloved Disciple had in fact died, and "his death had caused concern 'among the brethren' owing to the misunderstanding of the Lord's words in 21v22". This would of course mean that the Beloved Disciple was "a real individual, not an idealization of the ideal follower" (Carson pg681), as "one does not fret about the death of an idea" (Brown pg1119). Yet this is a view not shared by all (a notable example being Bultmann). Also if the death of the Beloved disciple had occurred, and Jesus had seemingly prophesied he would still be alive when Jesus came, presumably a reference to the Parousia, this would quite clearly diminish the authority of Jesus. Moreover, it might also diminish the standing of the Beloved Disciple if for example his followers, presuming there were some, had claimed immortality for the Disciple.

v24-25. It is initially indicated that 'this is the disciple', that is the

Beloved Disciple, who is the witness to the things written in the gospel (though some have taken his witness merely to be given to the events in this chapter). This would give authority to the material if the disciple Jesus loved attested to it. Immediately, though almost seeming as an afterthought, it is stated that the Beloved Disciple had actually 'written these things'. This would further strengthen the authority of the material.

There follows the attestation that 'we know that his testimony is true', and this "emphasis both on testimony (witness) and on its truth is characteristically Johannine." (Brown pg1124). This verse seems to be written by someone other than the disciple himself, perhaps by "elders of the church at Ephesus, others close to the beloved Disciple, or the church to which he belonged." (Carson pg683), adding a seal of approval (Brown pg1124). However, Carson (pg684) also notes that the 'we' may merely be an editorial 'we' and actually include within it the Beloved disciple himself.

The gospel then ends on a hyperbole (exaggeration), namely that if everything Jesus did was written about, and it is acknowledged there were other things than those written in the gospel, the whole world would not contain the books that could be written.

It should be noted that there are a number of similarities between John's account of the catch of fish in Chapter 21 and the call of the first disciples in Luke Chapter 5. Both events take place at the Sea of Galilee, and in both Jesus instructs that they should put down their nets. In Luke the instruction is specifically to Peter. In both accounts Peter informs Jesus that they have been fishing all night and have caught nothing. A great catch of fish is achieved in both passages and 'following' Jesus is a feature at the end of the two incidents. The sons of Zebedee (James and John) are in both incidents.

There are also differences. In Luke the fish were dragged into the boats, filling them and causing them to be in danger of sinking. Also Luke notes that the nets were breaking. Peter on seeing what is happening asks Jesus to depart for Peter himself is a sinful man. Jesus states that the disciples will become fishers of men.

John seems particularly keen to show the nets were not breaking perhaps because he desires to present a picture of unity and no schism within the churches. While Peter's comment about him being sinful is not spelled out in John, his presentation of the possible cleansing of Peter, and the disciple's need to reaffirm his love for Jesus after his denials, echo the picture of a sinner trying to make up for past mistakes.

Marsh suggests (pg657) that the two presentations are variant accounts of one actual occasion. As Luke 5 is based on Marcan material (1v16-20), though with Lucan additions, and both focus on the original calling of the earliest disciples, it seems likely that John has chosen to alter the original setting to make the account into a post-resurrection appearance. Yet John still shows the need to present a picture of discipleship and other desired activities of the disciples and church.

A summary of impressions of the appearance of Jesus by the Sea of Galilee

- A further example is given which shows that Jesus has risen from the dead.
- A great catch of fish is made possible because the disciples do as Jesus tells them.
- Peter makes amends for his previous denial of Jesus – he responds in rushing to be with Jesus, by dragging the fish to shore, by expressing his love for Jesus, and his future martyrdom is suggested.
- The Beloved Disciple may be shown to be superior to Peter – he recognises Jesus, follows Jesus, and acts as a witness to Jesus by writing the gospel.
- Characteristic features – Peter and the Beloved disciple, light and darkness, symbolism, the sacraments, love, discipleship, and witness.

SOME POSSIBLE PURPOSES OF THE PASSION AND RESURRECTION NARRATIVES

▶ 1. TO SHOW THE TRUE NATURE OF JESUS

The evangelist indicates in 20v30-31 that he has recorded Jesus' signs for a purpose. It may be that this purpose is uppermost in John's mind when he also records the events of the rest of the gospel, including the most important passion and resurrection narratives. This purpose is to enable the reader to identify Jesus as the Messiah and Son of God.

In terms of Jesus as Messiah, the evangelist wishes to show that Jesus is not to be seen merely as some political earthly Messiah. So he stops Peter fighting on his behalf in the garden and informs Pilate that he is no earthly king who threatens Roman rule, though king he is. His kingship is of and from above. On earth he demonstrates his messiahship as one of suffering, one who dies in fulfilment of his Father's scriptures. Jesus is sovereign and in control, but he is willing to lay down his life rather than fight to preserve it.

His relationship with the Father is as the Father's Son. The evangelist may wish to emphasise the true divinity of Jesus. Jesus uses the divine 'I am' in the garden and is crucified because as the Jews state, he had made himself God's Son. He has the power to rise from the dead and seems to be able to materialise and disappear at will. He has to ascend to the Father and Thomas confesses him to be 'my God'.

Yet the evangelist also wishes to show the true humanity of Jesus. He is taken and bound, flogged and presented to the crowd by Pilate as 'the man'. He is crucified, his body pierced by the spear, and he dies and is buried. Even the resurrected Jesus has hands and side that bear the marks of his experience on the cross.

(For a fuller discussion of the person of Jesus consult Booklet 5 in this series.)

▶ 2. TO EMPHASISE THE NEED TO 'BELIEVE'

The evangelist also records in 20v30-31 that he has recorded the work of Jesus so that people might 'believe' that Jesus is both Messiah and Son of God. In the garden Peter appears to believe in his master and is willing to fight on his behalf; yet Peter seems to believe in Jesus as some military king and the need to fight, and so the disciple's belief is misguided. Pilate may, through his meeting with Jesus ,come to the conclusion that Jesus is truly the king of the Jews. The testimony of the witness to the crucifixion events is to enable people to believe.

Joseph of Arimathea is a disciple and secret believer in Jesus; it may be that Nicodemus also believes. He has journeyed from the darkness of his first encounter with Jesus in Chapter 3, through encouraging the asking of questions about Jesus in Chapter 7, to taking and burying Jesus' body in Chapter 19.

The evangelist states that the Beloved Disciple 'saw and believed' through the empty tomb experience. Mary Magdalene after her initial lack of understanding believes Jesus has truly appeared to her and tells the disciples of her experience of the risen Jesus. It is implied that the disciples also believe in the resurrected Lord; this is true even of the doubting Thomas when Jesus appears while he is with his fellow disciples. Indeed Thomas' words of confession that Jesus is his Lord and God seem the pinnacle of appreciation and belief in Jesus. Yet Jesus praises more those future followers who will believe in him even though they will not have physically seen the resurrected Jesus.

For those who do believe the evangelist states (20v31) that they will be given life. In the Fourth Gospel this is 'zoe aionios', Greek for eternal life. This is more than a mere 'going on'; it is a qualitative experiencing of a relationship with Jesus and the Father.

▶ 3. TO INDICATE THE DESIRED NATURE OF DISCIPLESHIP

This aspect is clearly linked with 'believing' in Jesus. Yet for the evangelist discipleship means more than 'believing', it means giving allegiance to Jesus. It means demonstrating through word and actions that appreciation of what is necessary to be a true disciple. The path not to follow is indicated by the actions and words of both

Judas and Peter, though the later eventually shows commitment, the necessary love, and the willingness to risk death in 'following' Jesus.

Joseph and Nicodemus act courageously and without fear, and their great love for Jesus may be symbolised in the large quantity of spices they bring to anoint the body of the crucified Jesus. Mary Magdalene also shows her appreciation that Jesus is 'rabboni', and Thomas makes up for his doubting by acknowledging Jesus as Lord and God. Yet it is perhaps the Beloved Disciple who acts as the 'ideal' disciple, though even he is presented as real not perfect.

For Carson (pg657) Chapter 21 "is a quite independent fundamental and universal exposition of the nature of Christian discipleship and apostleship, and what it means in the need to 'follow Christ'." This same scholar (pg658) suggests that Chapter 21 brings to full and final expression all that the gospel wants the Christian to understand about the nature of discipleship.

▶ 4. TO PRESENT THE CHARACTERS OF PETER AND THE BELOVED DISCIPLE AND THEIR RELATIONSHIP

Both these disciples are key characters in the closing gospel narratives. Peter acted bravely in the garden to save his master from arrest, but his action was impetuous and misguided. While he followed Jesus into the High Priest's courtyard he then stands sharing the warmth of the charcoal fire with Jesus' opponents. Indeed, he needs later to be told by Jesus to follow him. He also acts in direct opposition to Jesus when he denies his master to protect himself. He runs to Jesus' tomb, at least not now with the opponents of Jesus, but his fellow disciple outruns Peter. It is Peter who, again impetuously, rushes into the tomb.

Up to the visit to the tomb, in contrast the Beloved Disciple's actions have been praiseworthy. He was with Jesus at the cross, and immediately obeyed Jesus' words that he should take Jesus' mother as his own. He outruns Peter to the tomb and respectfully hesitates before entering. When he does enter, the evangelist remarks that he 'saw and believed'.

It has been suggested that the evangelist's presentation of these two disciples was influenced by the situation at the time of writing, namely that certain churches were "inclined to exalt one over against the other." (Beasley-Murray pg410), and that "excessive partiality for Peter and John (the presumed Beloved Disciple) threatened schism in the Christian community." (Marsh pg655).

There is clear evidence in Paul's First Letter to the Corinthians of a tendency to divide into groups aligned with important figures within the Christian community. Paul in the Letter seems to battle against such divisions that might threaten to divide the Christian community; he aims to draw together the rival factions. Carson suggests (pg682) that the presentation of Peter and the Beloved Disciple in the Fourth Gospel is designed to similarly encourage unity and oneness.

Many scholars (e.g. Marsh pg655, Beasley-Murray pg411, and Strachan pg340) also argue that the evangelist does not seek to exalt Peter above the Beloved Disciple or vice-versa. However, the evidence examined within the gospel itself suggests that this point can be severely questioned. There does seem support that the Beloved Disciple has a certain "precedence over Peter" (Lightfoot pg 341). Peter often acts against the interests of Jesus, for which he is also often criticised. In contrast the Beloved Disciple acts in an ideal if not entirely 'perfect' manner.

It may be true that in Chapter 21 Peter is treated more sympathetically than elsewhere in the gospel. He is eager to reach Jesus on the shore, drags the fish onto the beach, and shares breakfast with Jesus. Further, he professes three times his love for Jesus, seemingly making amends for his previous denials, and his future martyrdom is indicated. The evangelist may be trying, by this presentation, to bring together those groups who aligned either with Peter or the Beloved Disciple.

It is possible that Chapter 21 was a later addition to the initial gospel that ended at 20v31. If this was so, it may be that Chapter 21 was added because immediately after circulation, John's Gospel met with opposition. This may have resulted in some rejecting John's testimony, and an ensuing division and potential schism within the Christian community. John or his church may have wished to ease the situation so that the gospel would be more readily acceptable and the division of Christians into either followers of Peter or the Beloved disciple would be prevented, or at least not cause some final schism.

Yet while the evangelist might be willing to compromise to establish unity, there is still below the surface in Chapter 21 some possible questions raised against Peter, and in contrast praise of the beloved Disciple. The latter recognises Jesus on the shore and follows Jesus without the need to be told to do so. Peter encourages a return to the old job of fishing, leaves the 'boat', possibly is shown to need cleansing, and can only offer Jesus 'philo' love not the Christian 'agape'. Peter is also told to focus on following not turning around.

It seems likely from Chapter 21v22-23 that the Beloved Disciple has now died. It may be that his death was what precipitated the need for Chapter 21 (Carson pg652). Clearly the evangelist wishes to clear up the misunderstanding and belief within the Johannine community that the Beloved Disciple would live until Jesus' second coming, the Parousia. If the Johannine community had publicised their mistaken belief, the "enemies of the gospel" (Carson 682) may well have smirked and gloated when the Beloved Disciple actually died. The correction may have been an attempt to diffuse the situation, and may have led to the supposed need to compromise on the presentation of Peter. Also the indication that, while Peter was to be a pastoral leader within the church the Beloved disciple had written the gospel, may have been to give authority and acceptability to the gospel.

(Those interested in further examining, from a general rather than a merely Johannine consideration, the aligning of churches with leading figures, should read Goulder's 'Tale of Two Missions'. Goulder examines the situation from the perspective of a Petrine and Pauline 'division'. John would have been within the Pauline school of thought.)

▶ 5. TO CORRECT AND SUPPLEMENT THE RECORD OF THE SYNOPTIC GOSPELS

This may have been a general desire of the evangelist in writing his gospel, though it would need John's awareness of the Synoptic Gospel's record to be strictly true, and all scholars do not agree on this. Within the passion and resurrection narratives, John has some fairly major differences when compared with the narratives of the Synoptic Gospels.

One such difference is his presentation of Jesus as commented on above. In particular John has presented a Jesus largely in control of proceedings and one of divine proportions. He also has different statements of Jesus from the cross.

The evangelist also adds considerable material with regard to Peter and the beloved Disciple, also commented on above.

Yet perhaps the most notable change in the Fourth Gospel is the dating of Jesus' crucifixion. According to the Synoptic Gospels, though the dating largely depends on Mark, Jesus is crucified on Nisan 15, which was Passover Day. Yet John suggests Jesus was crucified on Nisan 14 which was the day of Preparation for Passover. John repeats the dating so that there can be no doubt of his intention. Generally the purpose suggested is that John wished to theologically present Jesus' death at the same time the Passover lambs were being slaughtered, so that Jesus himself is identified as a replacement sacrifice, the new Passover lamb. It is also generally suggested that John's dating is not correct as he has been influenced by his theological desires. This may be so, though it could also be argued that Mark might have changed the dating as he wished to present Jesus as the Passover.

The main problem for the different churches would have been on which day was the crucifixion of Jesus to be remembered. It was a problem for worship and one which John may have felt so strongly about that his record needed to put straight the record of the Synoptic Gospels, or of the tradition surrounding Jesus' death.

▶ 6. TO ESTABLISH THE ACCEPTABILITY OF THE GOSPEL ITSELF

It is generally accepted that within the second century A.D. the Gospel of John was not readily accepted within Christendom. This may have been because of the differences within his presentation from that of the Synoptic Gospels or general traditions within Christianity as a whole. The evangelist may have perceived this might be a future problem when he wrote the gospel and so his record contains emphasis on truth and witness. If the opposition to the gospel came immediately it was produced and circulated, the evangelist may have edited his gospel to make it more acceptable.

Indeed this may have been the reason for adding, if this was the case, Chapter 21. The material in the chapter contains the indication (perhaps from the elders of the Johannine church) that Jesus' most special disciple, the Beloved Disciple was the witness behind that gospel and in fact the one who wrote it, which should give authority and acceptability to the gospel.

Moreover, if the record of the Synoptic Gospel's was linked with the witness of Peter, then John would have needed to show the worth of his gospel based as it was on the testimony of the Beloved Disciple. Also as suggested above, John may, in Chapter 21, have given a more authoritative presentation of Peter to ease any schism between the Petrine and Johannine communities.

▶ 7. TO PRESENT MATERIAL ABOUT THE CHURCH

The evangelist may have seen the disciples within his gospel as representative of the church. In the closing narratives the incidents seem to advance the requirements of discipleship (as above) expected presumably from those in the church at the time of the evangelist. In his appearances, Jesus states that he is sending out the disciples as he has been sent by his Father, thus indicating the apostolic role of the church. Jesus also gives the community his 'peace', and possibly more importantly, the Holy Spirit. He also establishes the authority of the church by stating that those within it as disciples have the power to forgive or retain sins. This means that a judgmental role is the prerogative of the church.

The pastoral role of Peter in looking after the lambs and sheep of the church may also be shown to indicate the importance in the "oversight of the practical life of the church" (Lightfoot pg341) of such a role within the Christian community. Similarly, the role of the Beloved Disciple as "witness and guardian of the Lord's revelation and of the truth of the gospel" (Lightfoot pg341) may show the importance of this activity for the future of Christianity. The two disciples may have "equally significant vocations" (Beasley-Murray pg417) for the church and its ministry.

The evangelist may have intended to symbolise the church by the boat in the final resurrection appearance, which in itself, as "the story of a

Galilean appearance", may have been used "to symbolise the work of the apostolic church" (Strachan pg335). The casting of the net and the catch of fish could be symbolic of bringing more into the Christian community. The tunic of Jesus that was not torn and the unbroken net could be symbols of the unity required within the church.

It has been suggested (e.g. by Goulder) that the purpose of the gospel as a whole may have been to help those who were going through a process of study in order to commit themselves to joining the church. Such 'students' were called catechumens preparing themselves for baptism and entry into the church, probably at Easter time.

There may be certain veiled allusions to baptism and the Eucharist in the passion and resurrection narratives. Both sacraments may have been intended in the 'blood and water' that flowed from Jesus side on the cross. The Eucharist may have been represented by the breakfast on the shore of the Sea of Galilee, and Peter's diving into its waters, representative of the baptism of the erring disciple.

The evangelist's presentation of the death of Jesus on Nisan 14, not Nisan 15 as in the Synoptic Gospels, may have reflected the situation within the Johannine church. A group who remembered Jesus' crucifixion on Nisan 14 were called the 'Quartodecimans' or the '14thers'. They seem to have been members of the Christian church in the area of Asia (Minor). John may have been a supporter of the group, and championing their practice in his gospel.

There may also be an example of creedal statements within the church in Thomas' confession of faith, as the disciple acknowledges Jesus as 'my Lord and my God'.

▶ 8. TO SHOW HOW SCRIPTURE WAS FULFILLED

In the passion and resurrection narratives the evangelist shows more interest than elsewhere in his gospel in recording the fulfilment of scripture. Such texts seem to act as 'proof texts', proving that all that is happening to Jesus is part of the plan of God. This similarly proves the connection of Jesus with those plans of his Father. In 19v24 the sharing of the garments may be linked with Exodus 28v32 and Psalm 22v18; 19v28 Jesus' thirst probably with Psalm 69v21; 19v36 Jesus not having any of his bones broken with Exodus 12v46, Numbers

9v12, and Psalm 34v20; 19v7 looking on one pierced with Zechariah 12v10.

The evangelist also indicates the fulfilment of certain of Jesus' words, which may be an attempt to show that Jesus shares the omniscience of God himself. In 18v9 Jesus' words are fulfilled in that he has not lost one, Peter's denials fulfil Jesus' earlier prophecy in 13v38, and in 18v32 acknowledgement is made of Jesus' appreciation of the death he was to die.

SYMBOLISM OR HISTORICITY?

In this booklet it has occasionally been suggested that John may have used symbolism; this is the use of details in an event or incident which are presented as a symbol of something else, generally from a theological or spiritual perspective. This would be similar to the suggestion that John's 'signs' were 'signposts' to be interpreted or 'followed' in order for the real significance of the sign to be appreciated. It is acknowledged that not all will agree or be persuaded that this is true for symbolism in the gospel.

It may be true that the Synoptic Gospels, and particularly St. Mark's Gospel, have been consider to have more right to be seen as historical than the more perceived spiritual gospel of John. However, this may in fact do a disservice to the Synoptic Gospels, which may also contain symbolism and theological significance within the events rather than merely be a record of events that happened.

Possible examples of details which may be symbolic in the Passion and Resurrection narratives of the Fourth Gospel include, the lanterns used in the garden, Jesus carrying his own cross, the blood and water which flows from Jesus in the cross, the catch of fish and the number caught, the unbroken net, and even the breakfast eaten beside the Sea of Galilee. Brown, for example, notes (pg791) that the episodes while Jesus is on the cross are "selected for their symbolic import and scarcely a detail has been included that is not theologically oriented."

Yet it is acknowledged that these details may be accurately recorded as being those seen within actual historical events. The crucifixion of Jesus is referred to in Josephus' historical writings, and this event itself would seem to be historical. Other historical details may include, for example, that it was Peter who cut off the ear of the High Priest's servant whose name may have actually been Malchus, Jesus may have been tried by Annas before he was sent to Caiaphas, Jesus may have been crucified on Nisan 14 not on Nisan 15 as the Synoptic Gospels record; John's 'tradition' could in fact be superior to that used for the Synoptic Gospels' dating. Also the side of Jesus may have been pierced by a javelin which caused a releasing of blood and water, and Jesus may have risen from the dead as was apparently witnessed in the days soon after he had been crucified.

The discussion before Pilate might be more difficult for some to accept, not merely because it is different from that recorded in the Synoptic Gospels, but because it was held in private between Pilate and Jesus. Yet some might argue that the resurrected Jesus or even the Holy Spirit might have told the disciples details of the conversation.

So, whether or not John's Passion and Resurrection Narratives are to be seen as historical or symbolic is hotly debated. It may of course be that the two features are not mutually exclusive, that symbolism might emerge from the historical. Marsh suggests (pg285) that even if certain details are presented for theological reasons there is "no need to reject the statement as unhistorical." The writer may have intended the event to be understood as historical but as also revealing some symbolical truth.

It would be hoped that an evangelist whose gospel frequently refers to witness and truth, with Jesus, as the 'I am' of truth, would be recording history as it happened. Yet it must also be appreciated that the evangelist did not merely set out to record facts (he was not a mere chronicler of events) or provide historical and biographical details about Jesus. He no doubt wished to convey theological and spiritual truths, as he saw them, which would have an impact on the destiny of the reader.

Our own interests and theological perspectives, or our disposition to see historically or symbolically, may likewise influence our interpretation of Johannine details. The evangelist does not indicate that he is using symbolism, but he may have done so, to bring about the believing which seems his intention according to Chapter 20v30.

John's material was no doubt written to help those who lived in his own historical time, faced with certain historical circumstances. Dealing with such circumstances may have led him to be influenced in his presentation of the evidence. Yet that does not mean that the message of the Gospel is not still dynamic and meaningful to readers in the twenty-first century. Narrative criticism, among its suggestions, generally highlights the importance of reader-response, what the events mean for today. Some may see John's record as of historical interest while others may wish to see more its worth and relevance. This seems to be the message of Marsh as he wrestles with the idea of what might be going on in what takes place.

The symbolism seen by people such as myself may possible be there, and there because the evangelist intended it so; however, it might not be there at all. Arguments will come and go, but at least one should be prepared as Marsh suggests (pg418) to "evaluate the evidence for himself."

WORKSHEET

1. Examine the presentation of Jesus in the garden and High Priest's courtyard incidents.
2. Consider the errors of appreciation shown by Peter in the garden and within his denials.
3. Do you consider John's treatment of Caiaphas as 'sympathetic'?
4. What can be learned about the person of Jesus from his trial before Pilate?
5. Do you consider there to be evidence to support the suggestion that the evangelist was
   (a) sympathetic to the Romans,
   (b) anti-Jewish?
6. Why did Pilate crucify a man he held to be innocent?
7. Consider the significance of Jesus' words from the cross.
8. Identify and consider the links with scripture of the crucifixion events.
9. Do you consider there to be evidence to support the suggestion that Nicodemus was a disciple of Jesus?
10. What may be learned about the person of Jesus from his resurrection appearance to Mary Magdalene?
11. Comment on the character of Thomas.
12. To what extent do you think there is sacramental material in Chapter 21?
13. Identify and consider the possible symbolism in Chapter 21.
14. Do you agree with the suggestion that the main aim of the evangelist in the resurrection appearances was to show the superiority of the Beloved Disciple over Peter?

EXAM QUESTIONS

The reason why most people fail exams at A/S, A Level, and above is because they write irrelevant information as opposed to inaccurate information. The plea of examiners is always "answer the question asked". However, students often regurgitate answers from questions set during their studies. Such 'model' answers are used irrespective of the slant or emphasis in the exam question.

It is also noted by examiners that students do not always seem to be aware of what is actually required by words used in questions. This is particularly true of such words as – discuss, assess, evaluate, and show how far you agree or disagree (with a view). Candidates frequently ignore the trigger words and instead set out on the task of writing all they know on a particular topic.

It is important that answers are planned before embarking on an essay answer. Not only does this allow a student to arrange material in a logical order, but this also serves as an 'early warning system' showing whether they have sufficient knowledge to fully answer the question. Plans for essays should be fairly brief; many candidates write very long plans often with the result that they fail to finish all questions on the examination paper.

One useful method to aid keeping to the required material is to highlight key words and phrases in the question.

The following questions test 'appreciation' of the key areas of:-

1. Purposes ('aims') of the Passion and Resurrection narratives.

2. The Person of Jesus in the Passion and Resurrection narratives.

3. Sacramental possibilities in the Passion and Resurrection narratives.

1. **"The main aim of the evangelist in his resurrection narratives was to encourage belief in the person of Jesus."**
   Examine and assess this view.

   The word 'examine' requires more than a mere indication of relevant passages. An answer needs to demonstrate knowledge and understanding, and any concepts need unpacking with relevant explanations and comments. Comments need to offer reasons, and the better answers will take note of relevant examples and illustrations to support the point made.

   The word 'assess' requires more than a one-sided opinion. An answer needs arguments both for and against any viewpoint expressed. The alternatives within the evidence need to be considered and comments may be included on both strengths and weaknesses of the various arguments. A conclusion will be expected.

   This particular question is about the purposes of the resurrection narratives. The view focuses on belief in relation to the person of Jesus.

   Passages linked with belief need to be referred to and 'examined'. Such passages would include: e.g. John's own statement in 20v30-31, opposition to Jesus from non-believers, question of Pilate's belief, crucifixion presented to bring about belief ((19v35), the Beloved Disciple sees and believes (20v8), Mary's belief after initial lack of appreciation, belief of disciples, lack of initial belief of Thomas, and his eventual confession of faith.

   Though the question is about purposes, the wording 'person of Jesus' means that brief comments about Jesus are creditworthy.

   Examination of other possible purposes is also needed, including e.g. particular focus on Jesus, the nature of discipleship, relationship of Peter and the Beloved Disciple, adding to Synoptic Gospel material, encouraging acceptance of the gospel itself, considering various church interests including the sacraments, and the fulfilment of scripture.

   Within the assessment of the view comments are needed on

'main'. Some attempt should be made to try to make some assessment of what was important to the evangelist, though an indication of difficulties in doing this could be stated. The weight of evidence needs considering, possibly the sheer number of indications of a specific area might be indicated. The importance might be judged on the weight of evidence not merely within the resurrection narratives but within the gospel as a whole.

Sometimes candidates only offer comments in support of the view expressed in the question. While such support is clearly needed, to ensure a debate takes place, a real effort should be made to argue against the view. It should be noted that the view does not necessarily have to be accepted. There should be a case to be made against the view, otherwise the question would not have been set.

Some attempt at a conclusion should be made even if the conclusion is that that there can be no absolute conclusion on the topic!

2. In the passion and resurrection narratives the evangelist presents a Jesus who is neither truly human nor truly divine."
Examine and assess this view.

See Q1 above for general comments on 'examine' and 'assess'.

The focus of this question is on Jesus within the passion and resurrection narratives. Passages indicating Jesus' humanity need 'examining'. Such passages would include: e.g. he is capable of being seized and bound, he can be struck, and he suffers flogging, mockery and crucifixion. Pilate refers to him as 'the man', and Jesus can bleed, die and is buried. His body bears the marks of the nails and spear, he can be touched, and also appears to cook breakfast by the Sea of Galilee!

Passages indicating Jesus' divinity need 'examining'. Such passages include: e.g. Jesus' knowingness, his 'I am', his heavenly kingship, his relationship with the Father, his ascension and resurrection, his apparent materialising, his power to dispense the Holy Spirit, and Thomas' acknowledgement that he is Lord and God.

In the assessment, comments may be made on 'truly' (what it means and what is needed for a judgement to be made) in relation to both the humanity and divinity of Jesus. Problems in judging or within the 'evidence' might be considered. Comment could be made on the evangelist's intentions in his presentation. For example, it would have been problematic to present a divine Jesus to some holding monotheistic views. Jesus' 'sonship' may not necessarily be an indication of divinity, merely of messiahship.

Support could be suggested for either not truly human or truly divine but not both, or truly human or truly divine but not both.

Remember to examine and assess not merely indicate points about Jesus.

---

3. "There is no sacramental material within the Johannine passion and resurrection narratives."

Discuss how far you agree with this assertion.

The word 'discuss how far' requires similar treatment indicated above in Q1 with regard to 'assess'. Knowledge and understanding will be shown in the arguments set out both for and against the assertion expressed. Yet also there is a need to consider the 'degree' (how far) of support or opposition to the view.

In an introduction reference may be made to the possibility that the evangelist is

a) concerned positively about the sacraments,
b) asacramental, showing no apparent interest in the sacraments,
c) concerned with the inner meanings of the sacraments,
d) anti-sacramental, deliberately avoiding reference to the sacraments.

Reference to scholarly material would aid the presentation

Introductory comments might also be presented on 'sacramental', and on baptism and the Eucharist in particular. It may be pointed out that in the Fourth Gospel there is no Institution of the Eucharist by Jesus nor is there a detailed description of Jesus' own baptism, though it is alluded to in 1v33-34, and reference is made to baptism by John the Baptist and Jesus' own disciples.

Possible veiled allusions to the sacraments should be presented from the passion and resurrection passages. References to baptism might include e.g. water flowing from Jesus' side on the cross, Peter in the Sea of Galilee, and the possible intention of the evangelist in showing Jesus baptising with the Holy Spirit (20v22). Reference to Eucharist might include e.g. blood (representative of the wine at Eucharist) flowing from Jesus' side (a 'body' link) on the cross, and the breakfast of bread and fish by the Sea of Galilee. (Comment may be made on the relevance of fish rather than wine in the breakfast meal).

To establish a 'general' picture brief reference might be made to relevant material outside the targeted passages, This might include reference in particular to material in Chapter 6 and in Chapter 13.

Consideration could be given to the possibility that there is reference to one of the sacraments but not both baptism and Eucharist, and remember the degree (how far) must be examined. Comments would need to be based on evidence presented, as would an expected conclusion on the topic.

FURTHER READING

The Gospel According to St John. By C. K. Barrett
(SPCK: First published 1955)
Readability *, Content # # # #.
Challenging and fairly conservative, yet a truly authoritative work.

John. By G. R. Beasley-Murray
(Word Publishing: U.K. Edition 1991)
Readability * *, Content # # #.
Some fair comments, when one has mastered the way the book is sectionalised.

The Gospel According to John (Vol 2). By R. E. Brown
(Doubleday: 1970)
Readability *, Content # # # #.
Expansive and full of most thoughtful and challenging scholarship.

The Gospel of John. By F. F. Bruce
(Pickering 1983)
Readability * *, Content # # #.
Sensible and considered comments

The Gospel According to John. By D. A. Carson
(IVP: First published 1991)
Readability * * *, Content # # # #.
A fine commentary, full of scholarly points

The Fourth Gospel and its Predecessor. By R. Fortina
(T & T Clark 1988)
Readability * * *, Content # #.
Clear comments on the salient points.

The Gospel of John. By K. Grayston
(Epworth: 1990)
Readability * * * *, Content # # #.
A very readable study, though fairly brief.

St John. By J. Marsh
(Pelican: First published 1968)
Readability * * *, Content # # #.
Some sensible and thought-provoking comments.

According to St John. By J. N. Sanders and B. A. Mastin
(Black 1968)
Readability * * *, Content # #.
A 'solid' commentary.

The Gospel According to St. John (Vol 3). By R. Schnackenburg
(Burns and Oates 1982)
Readability *, Content # # #.
A thorough and authoritative analysis of the narratives.

KEY   Readability   * manageable;   ** good;
                         *** very good;   **** excellent.

          Content   # adequate;   ## good;
                         ### very good;   #### excellent.

NOTES